Enriching Ideas
FROM A TO Z

Also by Linda Hoffman Kimball

Apple Pies and Promises
Chocolate Chips and Charity
Raspberries and Relevance
Home to Roost
The Marketing of Sister B.

Enriching Ideas
FROM A TO' Z

Written and Illustrated
by Linda Hoffman Kimball

CFI
Springville, UT

ISBN 13: 978-1-55517-965-7
ISBN 10: 1-55517-965-7

Published by CFI, an imprint of Cedar Fort, Inc., 925 N. Main, Springville, UT, 84663
Distributed by Cedar Fort, Inc., www.cedarfort.com

LIBRARY OF CONGRESS CATALOGING-IN-PUBLICATION DATA

Kimball, Linda.
    Enriching ideas from A to Z / by Linda Kimball.
    p. cm.
    Includes bibliographical references and index.
    ISBN 1-55517-965-7 (alk. paper)
    1. Mormon women--Religious life. 2. Relief Society (Church of Jesus Christ of
Latter-day Saints) 3. Mormon Church--Doctrines. 4. Church of Jesus Christ of
Latter-day Saints--Doctrines. I. Title.

    BX8641.K54 2006
    230'.9332--dc22

                            2006016377

Cover design by Nicole Williams
Cover design © 2006 by Lyle Mortimer
Printed in the United States of America

10 9 8 7 6 5 4 3 2 1

Printed on acid-free paper

Dedication

For my friend Ann Stone

Contents

Acknowledgments

Special thanks (in alphabetical order) to these people, who helped me in myriad ways: Janie Baskin, Kerstin Bean, Suzette Broome, Georgia Carpenter, Ellen Carter, Elizabeth DeSchryver, Sheila Duran, Ann Gadzikowski, Nancy Harward, Janna Haynie, Christina Kimball, Chris Kimball, Georgia Llamzon, Marci McPhee, Veneese Nelson, Michelle Purrington, Monica Rogers, Lindsey Shumway, Ann Stone, and Natalie Wainwright.

Introduction

Springboard, spark, generator: this book is all of these. Manual, all-inclusive, set in stone: this book is none of these.

Enriching Ideas from A to Z is the extended brainstorming session from one woman who cares about the power and promise of Relief Society. It also benefits from the wisdom of contributors who share their perspectives on how the new home, family, and personal enrichment program is working in their units so far. Primarily, this fun and faithful volume is a prompt for you. Start from here and expand into your own creative realms to meet the needs and desires of your sisters— and perhaps discover some new interests of your own!

So, ladies, let's have some fun!

Purposes and Possibilities of Home, Family, and Personal Enrichment

The general Relief Society presidency restructured the approach to home, family, and personal enrichment, effective as of January 1, 2006. We now have four ward-wide Relief Society enrichment "events" and other smaller activities and ongoing interest groups based on the needs and interests of the sisters in our wards.

In their guidelines, the general Relief Society leaders see the following purposes to the new home, family and personal enrichment program:

- Strengthen faith in Jesus Christ
- Teach parenting and homemaking skills
- Strengthen homes, families, and individuals
- Socialize
- Learn from each other
- Be uplifted

+ Provide these opportunities in a safe, relaxed, and engaging environment

The guidelines are great gifts. These broad, open-ended purposes allow for:

+ Creativity to address needs and interests of sisters in varied situations
+ Increased flexibility in schedule, outreach, format, and approach
+ Simplicity—a rare commodity in today's hectic world

As local Relief Society leaders planning activities, interests groups, and events, we can:

+ Foster spirituality, good will, and service among the sisters
+ Determine needs and wants of the women in our care
+ Match those needs and wants with activities
+ Strengthen families and individuals
+ Offer varied schedules
+ Encourage sisters to volunteer
+ Include and involve more sisters
+ Have the sisters come because they *want* to, not because they feel *compelled* to
+ Simplify—and enrich—the lives of women

As individuals participating in enrichment, we can:

+ Strengthen our faith in Christ
+ Socialize and have fun
+ Provide service in focused, productive ways
+ Become stronger individuals and family members
+ Share our talents with other sisters
+ Appreciate the talents of other sisters
+ Volunteer to lead or participate in groups
+ Learn something we always wanted to learn
+ Learn something we never knew we wanted to know
+ Invite and involve our friends
+ Come up with our own interests and pursue them
+ Determine what works best for our interests, family and schedule

- Eliminate guilt that comes with feeling "obligated"
- Simplify—and enrich—our lives

24/7 Guiding Principles

24 Principles for Planning Activities

1. Keep the purposes of home, family, and personal enrichment front and center.

If you keep the purposes and goals of this program in mind in all your planning, pondering, and praying, you will be on the right track.

2. Keep things simple.

Don't feel you need to have every interest group covered and every need met every month or even every year. Remember that as leaders you can only do so much. Prayerfully select a few interest activities to host and allow sisters to choose among them. One of the big advantages of this new system is that life can be simpler for everyone—including the women serving and leading with enrichment activities and events.

3. Consider your budget.

Be careful to offer opportunities that have little or no cost so that any interested sister can participate in at least *some* appealing activity. Make sure the ladies know when there will be out-of-pocket expenses. For example, if you have a dining out club, you may want to go to fancy restaurants. That's fine, but be clear that the cost for dining out is the responsibility of each participant and not springing out of the ward Relief Society budget. A luncheon group that different women host at their homes could provide a nominal cost option for those interested in a similar kind of culinary experience.

4. Foster sisterhood not "splinterhood."

Encourage the sisters to develop common ties rather than fracturing into cliques. We don't want any showdowns between the collections group and the clutter busters club. This is the thrill and the challenge of diversity of interests. Be sensitive to the beginnings of any "have" or "have not" attitudes and quash them as effectively and as quickly as possible.

5. It's got a lot to do with marketing!

Which class are you more likely to attend? "Polyps and Your Large Intestine" or "It Takes Guts: What You Need to Know but Were Afraid to Ask about Colon Health."

A catchy title can draw people in to the least likely topic. Be sure to advertise well and in advance when an activity is coming up.

6. Lift up.

Because one of the purposes of all home, family, and personal enrichment activities and events is to be uplifting, "interest group" or "enrichment activity" should not be neutral names for what are really "gossip and gripe groups."

7. Schedule with flexibility—to a point.

Interest groups often are more than one day events (as opposed to particular visits, field trips, lectures, or workshops). If yours is ongoing, schedule with flexibility—to a point. Don't be so flexible that you tie yourself in knots to find a date and time that will work for everyone. The stars rarely align themselves so nicely!

8. Numbers can be misleading.

Scheduling may not correspond to everyone's busy lives. Some topics may appeal to more people than others. Don't determine the success of a function solely on attendance. Keep your group open to newcomers, veterans, and occasional participants.

9. Reassess.

If the need your group intended to meet is no longer urgent, reassess. Don't be afraid to change direction or even cancel. Lots of folks may sign up for a mall walking club in January in the fresh glow of New Year's resolutions, but don't be surprised if interest dwindles by March.

10. Vary topics.

Topic flexibility is a good thing. Some groups have a different focus each time they meet. Keep in mind the adage that you can't please all the people all of the time. Just give it your best communal, prayerful shot.

11. Choose a point person for communication.

Each activity or interest group would benefit from a point person who knows when and where the next meeting will be, what the topic will be (if there is one), and can advertise this to the rest of the sisters. This could be the enrichment leader, a member of the enrichment committee, or some enthusiastic volunteer.

12. Guidelines can be helpful.

For the benefit of some interest groups, a few basic guidelines ("rules") could save trouble down the road. For example, a book group might expect its attendees to actually read the book. Does that work for your group? Maybe, maybe not. Punctuality is a useful rule for some kinds of activities. If you're heading out on a hike at precisely 4 P.M., you may not find it workable to wait for latecomers, or all of you may end up hiking back in the dark. Find out what will help your groups be as satisfying as possible for the participants.

13. Determine the interests and needs of the sisters.

Periodically—possibly annually depending on your circumstances—determine what kinds of things your sisters should and may want to know about. This can be accomplished through a written survey, telephone, e-mail, or whatever other creative method you come up with. Perk up your surveys with variations from time to time to keep the ladies on their toes.

14. Encourage sisters not to hide under bushels.

You may know Sister Snow as a fabulous bread baker, but did you know she has been training circus elephants for years? Be on the alert to the hidden talents in your ward and encourage the ladies to let their lights shine brightly.

15. One shot wonders are great!

Consider having a one-topic gathering. The opportunity to spend one night socializing and learning about "Eliza R. Snow; Poet, Pioneer, and President" could provide just the tonic for the sisters in your unit. Some women may not feel that ongoing interest groups work for them, but one night (or day) spent on a compelling topic could be perfect!

16. A series can be super.

Maybe your evening on Eliza R. Snow goes so well that

you decide to do a series on the lives of the Relief Society presidents. Go for it! Or, if you're in a particularly musically inclined ward, maybe you could have a series on the instruments your gifted sisters play. Or how about a series highlighting the local sports team for the sport that's in season?

17. A good teacher can make the most unlikely topic come alive.

If you feel an urgent need to address an issue with the sisters that is either complex, dull, or otherwise unappealing (Tax code changes? Medicare reform? Neglected personal hygiene?), select someone who is an excellent public speaker or an engaging teacher to address the topic. They will be more likely to deliver the message—whatever it is—with aplomb and persuasion.

18. Make this a guilt-free zone.

With the expansive view of this new enrichment program, sisters can choose among many options. While the four enrichment "events" per year are intended for all sisters to attend, sisters should be encouraged to choose for themselves how to participate in ways that will accomplish the goals of enrichment. Maybe the best way for some to "strengthen homes and families" is to stay home with their families! Judge not.

19. Broaden the circle.

If your non-member aunt is a specialist on the politics of the Middle East, why not invite her to address your next enrichment activity or event? Does your neighbor like to garden? Invite her to come with you to learn about perennials. Share the wealth and widen the circle!

20. Something for everyone.

One of the challenges of any enrichment occasion is finding ways to engage sisters who never or rarely attend church. Inviting them to lead a discussion or teach a skill may include and involve them. Broader-based activities like field trips, topics of general interest, or a service project might suit them better than something pointedly doctrinal.

21. Prepare and Delegate.

Once you have a schedule in mind for your activities—and especially the four larger events—start to organize, delegate, and prepare well in advance. Delegating tasks to others can be tricky for some people. The burden of doing everything by yourself to have it just so may take a toll on you and the people in your orbit, so be cautious about your control issues. There will inevitably be last-minute surprises, but "she who is prepared shall not fear." And while you're preparing and delegating, remember to think about what kind of childcare needs the sisters may have!

22. There is no manual.

One size does *not* fit all, so there can never be a survey, an approach, or a list of activities and events that will work for every sister in every circumstance. Our leaders know this and have entrusted us with great freedom and flexibility. This may be scary to some who really like the comfort of being told what to do. This nudge out of our comfort zones is just one more part of strengthening us as individuals. The new program is a gift—but it's not a gift that comes with an owner's manual.

23. If it ain't broke, don't fix it.

If your previous enrichment system was working swimmingly for all of your sisters, then you're ahead of the game. In your case there may just be some new labels given to tried-and-true successes.

24. Transportation is a factor.

Think about how sisters will get to the activities. If you plan something, are the sisters who would most likely attend going to be able to get there? If not, how can you solve that problem? Can you take the activity closer to them? Carpool and pick them up? Is public transportation available to them?

Since one of our directives is to extend effort to "involve all the sisters," this is a topic which some wards will need to address with care.

And here's one more that refuses to be wedged into a tidy 24:

THINK OUTSIDE THE BOX

Enrichment activities and interest groups don't require a guest speaker (but they could have them), any formal instruction (but they might provide that), or even refreshments. (What? No refreshments?) Interest groups and activities don't have to have any more structure or content than just convening somewhere to sit together if that is what draws the ladies together and fills their wants and needs. (Lots of wards have knitting clubs. Yours could have a sitting club!)

7 Pointers for Planning Events

Here are seven points to keep in mind that specifically relate to the four events intended for all the sisters in the ward.

1. Plan the year.

Work with your presidency or committee to plan (or at least sketch out) all four events. Having a long view will provide you peace of mind and a good structure to build on as the selected dates approach.

2. Communicate with your priesthood leaders.

Counsel with your bishop or priesthood leaders concerning your plans. They may have useful perspectives to incorporate in your process. This also is a good route to make sure your events get in the ward calendar without scheduling conflicts. The more the Relief Society participates in executive council

meetings and personal priesthood interviews, the more uni-
fied the ward will be.

3. Multifaceted service projects.

Some of the most enriching enrichment occasions in the
past have been service projects with several parts. Magic hap-
pens when women can work on a common goal at the same
time. Some wards have created pillows for children having
medical procedures; others have assembled school bags for the
Church's humanitarian aid service, which included sewing the
fabric and putting the supplies in. Other examples abound.
These kinds of activities work well for large groups (Linda
Hoffman Kimball, *Raspberries and Relevance: Enrichment in
the Real World* [Springville, Utah: CFI, 2004]).

4. Food always brings people together.

At the four enrichment events, sisters will always appreciate having something to nibble or feast on. You don't have
to go whole hog (although, come to think of it, a luau theme
could be fun!), but it seems to be a given that if you feed them,
they will come.

5. Support the stake enrichment meetings.

With the guidelines for our current home, family, and
personal enrichment program is the note that the stake Relief
Society will sponsor one or two stake enrichment meetings
that will be planned at the stake level. One of these should be
held in conjunction with the annual broadcast of the general
Relief Society meeting. Be sure to advertise them in your local
units as they occur and support them with your attendance
whenever possible.

6. Events build unity.

While your array of interest groups and activities will
reach sisters who share common interests, an advantage of
hosting four events is to capitalize on common ground.

7. Spiritual boost.

In league with building unity through events is the ripe opportunity to give an extra measure of spirituality at these gatherings. If there's one thing we ought to have in common, it should be the desire to follow the Savior. With whatever other projects or fun you have planned for an event, it is always good to permeate the gathering with the Spirit. This is what distinguishes Relief Society from the woman's club or the park district's class offerings.

Making the Most of the A–Z Sections

If this book has any similarity to a manual, it is in giving you some how-to approaches to brainstorming. The following sections follow formats you can try on your own.

1. Sketch out topics broadly and quickly. My A–Z Bare-Bones list shows things that came to *my* mind. It probably lacks—to your utter astonishment—significant other topics like cryptography or flying machines or disability access. Feel free to pencil them in.

2. As with all brainstorming, don't pounce on everything you write with a critical eye and the attitude of "that's a stupid idea." That harsh editorial voice needs a time out for this kind of process!

3. Take a breather. Once you've listed whatever comes into your head, go for a walk, take a nap, legislate that bill, or carry on with whatever else is going on in your life. This will give

you some fresh perspective on your list when you approach it again.

4. Come back to your list and kindly, gently assess and sort. Maybe once you take another look you will see that some suggestions are less appropriate than others for your current purposes. (No, they are still not stupid ideas.)

5. Working from the structure you've just sketched out, subdivide and add details. Things should still be pretty loose at this level. The section called "A–Z Taking Shape" demonstrates this. Same thing goes:

+ Get your ideas down quickly
+ Take all comers without judging them harshly
+ Take a break
+ Assess and sort

6. Once you've started to get more homed in on topics, try whipping out a few specifics, adding a little more flesh to the bones, so to speak. Use a title, if that's a technique that works for you. This is what the section "A–Z with Curves" shows. Or you can always just write down the kernel of a lesson or activity and leave the catchy title to someone else on your committee. You'll see that I've come up with titles, but I leave all the subsequent planning and details to you! (You didn't think I'd take all the fun away from you, did you?)

7. Once you have a lot of ideas to work with you may want to sort them again. This time you may want to use different kinds of categories. In my "A–Z's by Welfare Wheel Topics" I decided to use the broad (and often overlapping) categories used by the Church's welfare system. Many wards use this in planning their activities. Depending on your circumstances, you might want to take the ideas you have and divide them into categories like: outdoor activities; activities that cost money; activities best held in homes; seasonal activities, and so on. The point is to give yourself some basic structure so your ideas don't become overwhelming.

8. If thinking by topic stumps you, and subdividing into categories seems to have you blocked, you could also try the A–Z technique and just let the alphabet be your prompt. Let the ideas come in no particular *topic* order at all. That's what I demonstrate in the "A–Z Potpourri" section. Again, you can pick and choose among your ideas once you've generated them.

A–Z Bare-Bones Topics

To get your own imaginative juices flowing, here are a few bare-boned possibilities. These suggestions are meant to spark your own creativity based on the needs and interests of your sisters.

- Animals
- Antiquing
- Art
- Archaeology
- Architecture
- Books
- Career building
- Cars
- Children and parenting
- Collections
- Cooking

- Community service
- Computers and technology
- Crafts
- Current events
- Dining out
- Drama
- Etiquette
- Fashion and beauty
- Financial fitness
- Games
- Gardening
- Health
- History
- Home repair and improvement
- Humanitarian service
- International
- Languages
- Movies
- Museums
- Music
- Nature and science
- Photography
- Physical fitness
- Spirituality
- Travel
- Urban exploration
- Women's studies
- Writing
- X-ray and radiation advances
- Young at heart and staying that way
- Zoos

A-Z Topics Taking Shape

To kick it up another notch, here are elaborations on some of the broad topics mentioned in the previous pages.

Animals:

- Bird watching
- Dog walking
- Exotic animals
- Livestock and large mammals:
  Goats
  Horses
  Pigs
  Sheep
- Pets:
  Birds
  Cats

Fish
Dogs
Rabbits
+ Poultry
+ Service animal training
+ Veterinary concerns
+ Wildlife in your area

Antiquing:

+ Appraising
+ Conserving
+ Hunting

Archaeology

Art:

+ Art history
+ Book illustration
+ Ceramics
+ Collage
+ Drawing
+ Graphic design
+ Fiber arts
+ Jewelry
+ Metals
+ Mosaic
+ Painting:
    Acrylics, oil, watercolor
+ Pastels
+ Pencil
+ Printmaking
+ Sculpture
+ Stained glass
+ Woodworking

Architecture:

- Civic planning
- Environmentally friendly advances
- Field trips and tours
- Identifying architectural styles
- History of architecture
- House design
- Local notable buildings

Books:

- Authors
- Book binding
- Fiction:
    - Children's literature
    - Humor
    - Mystery
    - Novels
    - Short stories
- History of Literature
- Non-fiction:
    - Biography
    - Essay
    - Feature writing
    - How-to
    - Inspirational

Career building:

- Asking for a raise
- Being an effective boss
- Being an effective employee
- Child care issues on the job
- Competitive computer skills
- Interviewing skills
- Language skills for the workplace
- Negotiating in the workplace

- Résumé workshops
- Retirement and benefits
- Telephone skills
- Tension on the job
- Unions and labor history

Cars:

- Antique and vintage
- Learning to drive
- Makes and models
- Maintenance and repair

Children and parenting:

- Aging parents
- Baby basics
- Balancing career and family
- Birthday party planning
- Developmental stages
- Educational advocacy
- Family home evening planning for all stages
- Grandparenting
- Health concerns
- Missionary moms
- Mom and tot time
- Money management for children
- Parenting tips
- Playgroups
- Prenatal primer
- School options
- Single mom support
- Special needs and gifted children
- Teaching children about sex and other values
- Teenagers

Collections

Cooking:

- Baking:
    - Breads
    - Cakes and cookies
    - Casseroles
- Blenders and juicers
- Breakfasts
- Campground cooking
- Canning
- Cooking for crowds
- Convection ovens
- Crock pots
- Desserts
- Eggs
- Entertaining
- Fruits
- Grains
- Herbs and oils
- Kitchen basics
- Low-fat meals
- Marinades
- Meals missionaries can make
- Meats
- Mixes
- Nutrition basics
- Pasta
- Refrigeration and freezing
- Soups
- Specialized diet cooking
- Stovetop
- Table settings
- Vegetables

Community service:

- Educational opportunities
- Gardens

- Health-based opportunities
- Homeless shelters
- Immigration
- Mentoring
- Soup kitchens
- Volunteering

Computers and technology:

- Basic computer-speak
- Digital equipment
- Gadgets
- Internet
- Overcoming technophobia
- Search engines
- Software/hardware
- Word processing

Crafts:

- Baskets
- Batik
- Beading
- Book binding
- Candles
- Card making
- Decoupage
- Dyes
- Flowers
- Handwork:
    Crocheting
    Cross-stitch
    Embroidery
    Knitting
    Quilting
- Leatherwork
- Papercrafts
- Pillows
- Rubber stamps

- Scrapbooking
- Tole painting
- Weaving

Current events:

- International
- Local
- National

Dining out:

- Holiday and themed luncheons
- Local restaurants

Drama:

- Acting and actors
- History of theater
- Improvisation
- Musical theater
- One-act plays
- Plays and playwrights
- Productions
- Readers theater
- Shakespeare
- Theater tours

Environmental issues:

- Building "green" structures
- Community-supported agriculture
- Hybrids—plants and vehicles
- Latest government environmental initiatives
- Organic gardening
- Recycling
- Renewable resources
- Planet-friendly practices

Etiquette

Family history/genealogy:

- Detective work from sources
- Family history libraries
- Family reunions
- Forms
- Gathering what you have
- Interviewing relatives
- Pedigree charts
- Photographs
- Recording stories
- Research techniques
- Reunion planning
- Societies
- Sources
- Submitting for ordinance work

Fashion and beauty

Financial fitness:

- Auctions
- Bargain hunting
- Coupon clipping
- Children and money
- Creating a budget
- Debt management
- Estate, garage, and yard sales
- Estate and will planning
- Investment strategies
- Job hunting
- Living within your means
- Online shopping
- Planning ahead
- Retirement

+ Taxes
+ Tithing

Fire safety

Games:

+ Board games
+ Children's games:
    Finger plays
    Jump rope chants
    Sidewalk games
+ Magic tricks and illusions
+ Juggling
+ Puzzles:
    Crossword
    Jigsaw
    Sudoku
    3-D

Gardening:

+ Annuals
+ Bulbs
+ Community gardens
+ Desert gardens
+ Flower gardens
+ Herbs
+ Orchards and fruit trees
+ Organic gardens
+ Perennials
+ Pest protection
+ Planter ideas
+ Rooftop gardens
+ Soil types
+ Terrariums

Health:

- Abuse protection
- Addictions
- Anatomy
- Basic first aid
- Birth defects
- Bones
- Breast health
- Cancer support and survivors
- Cardiac health
- Children's health issues
- Colds, flu, and remedies
- Colon health
- "Do Not Resuscitate" and other hospital instructions
- Drugs
- Eye health
- Fire prevention
- Foot health
- Gerontology
- History of medicine
- Hospice
- Infertility/fertility issues
- Male health concerns
- Massage
- Menstruation and menopause
- Mental health:
  - Addictions
  - Counseling
  - Depression
  - Eating disorders
  - Suicide
- Nutrition
- OBGYN issues
- Plastic surgery
- Poison prevention
- Prenatal health/nursing/post-partum concerns
- Pulmonary health

History:

- Church history
- Local and community history
- World history

Home repair and improvement:

- Basic maintenance
- Clutter control
- Equipment
- House design
- Interior design
- Paint and paper
- Remodeling basics
- Short cuts that work
- Storage ideas
- Tile
- Tools

Humanitarian service:

- International opportunities
- Local opportunities
- National opportunities
- Practical tips for charitable giving

International:

- Cultures around the world
- Ethnic food
- International current events
- Worldwide humanitarian interests

Language:

- English as a second language
- Foreign languages
- Grammar and linguistics

+ Public speaking
+ Sign language
+ Tips for church talks
+ Word games

Movies

Museums

Music:

+ Contemporary music styles
+ Classical masterpieces
+ Composers
+ Jazz and blues
+ Music around the world
+ Music history
+ Music theory
+ Performing arts:
    Instrumental performance
    Choral performance

Nature and science:

+ Agriculture
+ Astronomy
+ Botany
+ Chemistry
+ Camping
+ Fire prevention
+ Environment
+ Geology
+ Hikes and trails
+ Horticulture
+ Marine life
+ Weather
+ Wildlife

Personal development:

- Communicating what you really mean
- Dealing with disappointment
- Developing trust
- Education
- Goal setting
- Journaling
- Leadership skills
- Overcoming fears
- Time management

Photography:

- Cameras and how they work
- Computer programs
- Digital advances
- Developing and printing
- Family portraits
- Studying the masters
- Tips for taking great photos

Physical fitness:

- Aerobics
- Badminton
- Bicycling
- Calisthenics
- Dance
- Fencing
- Gardening
- Gymnastics
- Hiking
- Jogging/running
- Martial arts/self-defense
- Pilates
- Ping-pong
- Pool

- Riding
- Rock climbing
- Rollerblading
- Ropes
- Snow sports:
    - Skating
    - Skiing
    - Sledding
    - Snowboarding
    - Snowman building
- Stretching
- Team sports:
    - Basketball
    - Soccer
    - Softball
    - Volleyball
- Walking
- Water sports:
    - Boating
    - Surfing
    - Swimming
    - Waterskiing
- Yoga

Spirituality:

- Church history
- Comparative religions
- Conference talks
- Exemplary women of faith
- Missionary matters
- Part-member families
- Prayer
- Scripture reading
- Service
- Temple visits

Travel:

- Day trips
- Exotic destinations
- Family vacations
- Local treasures
- Romantic getaways
- Planning tips

Urban exploration:

- City history
- Fun places to discover
- Food pantries and shelters
- Neighborhoods
- Local government
- Public transportation
- Security
- Walking tours

Women's Studies:

- Claiming our divine heritage
- Discovering our strengths
- Education through the ages
- Great women exemplars
- Families throughout history
- Relief Society through the years
- Suffrage history
- Women in the workforce

Writing:

- Children's literature
- Getting published
- Journalism
- Magazine pieces
- Manuscript critique groups
- Memoir and journals

- Novels
- Opinion pieces
- Poetry
- Short stories
- Travel writing

X-ray and radiation advances

Young at heart and staying that way

Yuletide planning

Zoos

A–Z with Curves

Ready for a little more embellishment? This time I've added not just a little meat to the bones, but some extra "flesh" to make it curvy. I took the previous framework and came up with titles for lessons or individual activities. If you want to do an ongoing series, you could select a few of your favorites (or come up with your own, of course!) and do them sequentially.

Animals:

- **Bird watching**—Winged and Wading Wonders: Identifying Flamingos, Herons, and Cranes
- **Dog walking**—A New Leash on Life: Starting Your Own Dog-Walking Service
- **Exotic animals**—Pythons on Parade: Snakes and Constrictors as Pets

- **Livestock and large mammals**—Horses for the Hapsburgs: The History of the Elegant Lipizzan Stallions
- **Pets**—Pint-Sized Pets: Hamsters, Gerbils, and Mice
- **Poultry**—If It Walks like a Duck: Care and Feeding of Domestic Fowl
- **Service animal training**—Dogs for the Deaf: Training Service Animals for the Hearing Impaired
- **Veterinary concerns**—Just a Fat Cat?: Distinguishing Symptoms That Need a Vet's Attention
- **Wildlife in your area**—Coyotes on Broadway?: Animal Predators in Urban Areas

Antiquing:

- **Appraising**—Road Shows without Rehearsals: Appraising Our Antiques
- **Conserving**—Brittle Bundles: Preserving Our Heirlooms
- **Hunting**—Gems among the Junk: Finding Antiques at Garage and Estate Sales

Art:

- **Art history**—Jan Vermeer: Master in the Dutch Golden Age
- **Book illustration**—Explosion of Styles: Caldecott Award Winners of the Last Fifty Years
- **Ceramics**—Throwing Yourself into It: Potter's Wheel Basics
- **Collage**—Cut, Paste, Create: Creating Art with All Kinds of Stuff
- **Drawing**—Eye Smarts: Designing a Pleasing Composition
- **Graphic design**—Make it Pop: Using Color Theory to Your Advantage
- **Fiber arts**—Spinsters Unite!: Learning to Use a Spinning Wheel
- **Jewelry**—Bead-decked and Bead-dazzled: Beading for Beginners

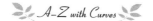

- **Metals**—Working with Silver: The Technique of Lost Wax Casting
- **Mosaic**—Chips and Chunks of China: Creating Mosaic Works of Art
- **Painting: acrylics, oil, watercolor**—Brush Up on Painting: Selecting the Correct Tools for Your Medium
- **Pastels**—Portraits That Come Alive: Shadows and Planes
- **Pencil**—Afraid of the Dark?: Getting Deep Tones in Your Black and White Work
- **Printmaking**—Spud Spectacular: Potato Print Gift Wrap and Greeting Cards
- **Sculpture**—Fun with Fimo: Working with Polymer Clay
- **Stained glass**—Color and Texture: Selecting Which Glass to Use
- **Woodworking**—Awl or Nothing?: Becoming Familiar with Woodworking Tools

Archaeology:

- **Boston's Big Dig:** Modern Archeological Discoveries

Architecture:

- **Civic planning**—Wide Enough to Turn a Team: Brigham Young's Salt Lake City
- **Environmentally friendly advances**—Let the Sun Shine: Practical Solar Panels
- **Field trips and tours**—The Charles Dawes House: Welcome to the Evanston Historical Society
- **Identifying architectural styles**—Ranch, Prairie, or Victorian: What Style is Your House?
- **History of architecture**—Cabins to Mansions: Early Styles in American Architecture
- **House design**
- **Elegant entryways**
- **Local notable buildings**—A Visit to the Lion House, Saturday, October 10. Meet there at 10 A.M.

Books:

- **Authors**—Flannery O'Connor and Literature of the South
- **Book binding**—In a Bind: Comb, Coil, and Wiring Binding Techniques
- **Fiction**—Agatha Christie and the Miss Marple Mysteries
- **History of literature**—Sturm und Drang: 18th Century German Literature
- **Non-Fiction**—Eleanor Roosevelt: Her Life and Times

Career building:

- **Asking for a raise**—Worth Every Penny: How to Ask for a Raise
- **Being an effective boss**—Gospel Principles of Leadership that Apply in the Workplace
- **Being an effective employee**—An Honest Day's Wage: Being an Effective Employee
- **Child care issues on the job**—Safe and Secure: Considerations for On-site Childcare
- **Competitive computer skills**—The Mouse Race: Keeping Your Computer Skills Up-to-Date
- **Interviewing skills**—Research and Eye Contact: Landing the Job through the Interview
- **Language skills for the workplace**—CEO, IPO, M-O-U-S-E: Learning "Compan-ese"
- **Negotiating in the workplace**—Beyond the Suggestion Box: Expressing Your Job Concerns Persuasively
- **Résumé workshops**—Résumé Writing: Job Skills Learned through Church Callings
- **Retirement and benefits**—What's Covered?: Understanding Your Benefits Package
- **Telephone skills**—What Do These Buttons Do?: Bonding with Your Cell Phone

- **Tension on the job**—What to Do when You Have a Boss from Heck
- **Unions and labor history**—Going Down: Coal Mine Strikes and Safety

Cars:

- **Antique and vintage**—Rah! Rah! Rumble Seats!: Antique Cars and Horseless Carriages
- **Learning to drive**—Standards Night: Learning to Drive Stick Shift in the Ward Meetinghouse Parking Lot
- **Makes and models**—Mazda or Model T: Differences between Car Makes and Models
- **Maintenance and repair**—Tran$mi$$ion Problems to Watch Out For

Children and parenting:

- **Aging parents**—Struggling in the Middle: Caring for Parents as well as Children
- **Baby basics**—Baby Basics: What to Expect during Your First Week at Home
- **Balancing career and family**—The Revolving Door: Creating Time to Be Together
- **Birthday party planning**—No Ponies Needed: Simple Birthday Parties with Less Stress
- **Developmental stages**—Boys are Stupid; Girls are Gross: Are My Children Sexist?
- **Educational advocacy**—Mainstreaming or Special Education: What's the Best for My Child?
- **Family home evening planning for all stages**—Short, Sweets, and to the Point: Strategies for Successful Family Nights
- **Grandparenting**—Spoil Them and Send Them Home?: Connecting with your Grandchildren
- **Health concerns**—Managing Migraines

- **Missionary moms**—Care Packages for Your Serving Sons and Daughters
- **Mom and tot time**—Picture Book Favorites: Story Time for Moms and Tots
- **Money management for children**—How Much is a Tooth Worth?: Teaching Children about Money and Molars
- **Parenting tips**—Help! My Angel has Turned into a Devil!
- **Playgroups**—Gross Motor Gatherings: Ackerman Park, Wednesdays at 9 A.M.
- **Prenatal primer**—Pregnancy Month by Month: Valuable Information for First-Time Moms
- **School options**—Public, Private, or at Home?: Pluses and Minuses of Each
- **Single mom support**—Single Moms: Carving Out Time for Yourself
- **Special needs and gifted children**—My Child the Nerd: Socializing Brilliant Children
- **Teaching children about sex and other values**—Some Are Fancy on the Outside: Body Awareness for Toddlers
- **Teenagers**—Sleep Deprivation and Early Morning Seminary: Facts and Strategies

Collections:

- **A Trip around the World:** Coins of Many Countries

Cooking:

- **Baking: breads, cakes, cookies and casseroles**—Nothin' Says Lovin': Visiting Teaching Treats from the Oven
- **Blenders and juicers**—Keep a Lid on It: Secrets to Blender Success
- **Breakfasts**—Nostalgia: Hot Breakfasts Like Grandma Made

- **Campground cooking**—Dutch Oven Delights!
- **Canning**—Jewels in Jars: Canning Peaches
- **Cooking for crowds**—Lotsa Lasagna: Italian Food for the Whole Huge Family
- **Convection ovens**—What's the Difference?: Basics of Convection Oven Cooking
- **Crock-Pots**—Slow Cooking Sweetness: Puddings and Desserts in the Crock-Pot
- **Desserts**—Pie-o-My-o-My!
- **Eggs**—The Yolks on You: Egg White Creations
- **Entertaining**—Elegant Entertaining from Linens to Lamb Chops
- **Fruits**—Appealing Apricots: Recipes Sure to Please
- **Grains**—Eye on Rye: Baking Rolls and Breads with Rye
- **Herbs and oils**—Basil and Balsamic: Easy Dipping Recipes to Try
- **Kitchen basics**—Measuring Spoons and Mixing Bowls: Standard Supplies for Your Kitchen
- **Low fat meals**—Great Grilled Vegetables!
- **Marinades**—Making Meats Tender and Savory with Marinades
- **Meals missionaries can make**—Five-Star Ramen Noodles Recipes
- **Meats**—What Cut is What: Studying the Butcher's Chart
- **Mixes**—Lemon Meringue Cake: A Mix Mystery Special
- **Nutrition basics**—Beyond Beans: Getting Enough Protein in Tasty Ways
- **Pasta**—Outrageously Good Orzo
- **Refrigeration and freezing**—How Long Will This Keep?: Freezing Food Basics
- **Soups**—Clam Up: New England and Manhattan Clam Chowders
- **Specialized diet cooking**—A Gluten-Free Life Made Easier

- **Stovetop**—Stovetop Cooking: Tasty One-Dish Meals
- **Table settings**—Which Way Does the Knife Edge Point?: Basic Table Settings
- **Vegetables**—Patio Tomatoes that Taste Terrific

Community service:

- **Educational opportunities**—The ABC's of Helping Children Read
- **Gardens**—Plant a Garden; Grow a Village
- **Health-based opportunities**—Comfort Kits for Chemotherapy
- **Homeless shelters**—For Every Bed a Blanket
- **Immigration**—Becoming a Citizen: How to Start
- **Mentoring**—Keeping Kids Active After School
- **Soup kitchens**—Ladling Love: Soup Kitchen Volunteer Experiences in our Town
- **Volunteering**—Snapdragons and Seniors: Planting Flowers at the Senior Center

Computers and technology:

- **Basic computer-speak**—Download and Delete: Basic Jargon to Know
- **Digital equipment**—Retrieving Your Digital Photos
- **Gadgets**—Global Positioning System: A Wife's Best Friend
- **Internet**—Handle with Care: The Fabulous World of the Internet
- **Overcoming technophobia**—Line upon Line Works for Computers, Too!
- **Search engines**—Giggle, Gaggle, Google!: Searching on the Internet
- **Software/hardware**—Megabytes and Major Bucks: Computer Systems and Setups
- **Word processing**—Hooray for Spell Check!: Word Processing Wonders

Crafts:

- **Baskets**—Thanksgiving Cornucopia Ideas to Be Thankful For
- **Batik**—Wax On, Wax Off: Fabric Art with Batik
- **Beading**—Beaded, Beautiful Bling!: Beaded Jewelry for Beginners
- **Candles**—Scented Candles for Christmas
- **Card making**—Pop-up Greeting Cards You Can Make at Home
- **Decoupage**—Transforming That Tabletop: Decoupage for Furniture
- **Dyes**—Not Too Young to Dye: Tie-Dying Socks and T-Shirts
- **Flowers**—Long-Stemmed and Lovely: Arranging Roses
- **Handwork: Crocheting, Cross-Stitch, Embroidery, Knitting, Quilting**—Keeping Them in Stitches: Weekly Handwork Gatherings
- **Leatherwork**—Tooling Leather Like a Pro
- **Papercrafts**—Pouring Paper: Basics of Handmade Papermaking
- **Pillows**—Quillows: Part Quilt, Part Pillow—All Fun!
- **Rubber stamps**—Powders and Paints: Basic Equipment for Rubber Stamping
- **Scrapbooking**—Storing These Treasures: Where to Put Them When I'm Done?
- **Tole painting**—Tole Painting: Learning the Crafts of Our Scandinavian Ancestors
- **Weaving**—Warp, Woof, and Wool: Setting Up a Navajo Loom

Current events:

- **International**—The Middle East and the Economics of Oil
- **Local**—Community Conservation Efforts
- **National**—Cell Phones and Highway Safety

Dining out:

- **Holiday and themed luncheons**—Valentine's Brunch, February 14, from 11 A.M. to 1 P.M. at Sister Smoot's
- **Local restaurants**—Girls' Night Out: Monthly Dinners at Downtown Restaurants

Drama:

- **Acting and actors**—Denzel Washington: A Man to Watch
- **History of theater**—Around the Globe: Exploring Shakespeare's Globe Theater
- **Improvisation**—Side-Splitting Sisters Improv Group—Monthly, First Saturday, 7–9 P.M.
- **Musical theater**—"Fiddler on the Spoof": Creating Our Own Musical
- **One-act plays**—Writing Our Own: Writing and Producing One Acts—a Three-Month Adventure
- **Plays and playwrights**—He's No Coward: Noel Coward's Comedies
- **Readers theater**—Pioneer Journals: A Reader's Theater May 1, 7–8 P.M., Cultural Hall
- **Shakespeare**—The Scottish Play: *Macbeth* and Its Lore
- **Theater tours**—Backstage Tour at the Regency Theater, June 22, 4 P.M.

Environmental issues:

- **Building "green" structures**—Warm and Friendly: Environmentally Sound and Effective Home Insulation
- **Community supported agriculture**—C.S.A.s: Finding or Founding an Organization near You
- **Hybrids: plants and vehicles:**
  Clementines: Where Do These Tasty Citrus Fruits Come From?

Biodiesel and Hybrid Cars: Vehicles of the
Future . . . or the Present?

* **Latest government environmental initiatives**—
Water Rights and Our State Laws
* **Organic gardening**—The Problem of Pests: Solutions
in Organic Gardening
* **Recycling**—Paper or Plastic?: A Bigger Question
Than You Think
* **Renewable resources**—Turnaround Trees: Natural
and Artificial Reforestation
* **Planet friendly practices**—Compost and
Conservation: What You Can Do

Etiquette:

* **The Lost Art of Thank You Notes**

Family history/genealogy:

* **Detective work from sources**—Clues from the Obits:
Discovering Ancestors in Odd Ways
* **Family history libraries**—Field Trip to the Family
History Library, Saturday, July 6, 10–12 A.M.
* **Family reunions**—The Gains and Strains of Family
Reunions
* **Forms**—Whose Name Goes Where on a Family
Group Sheet?
* **Gathering what you have**—The Sacred in the Shoe
Box: How I Met My Ancestors
* **Interviewing relatives**—Beyond Yes and No:
Questions to Get Them Talking
* **Pedigree charts**—Line upon Line: What Twelve
Generations Looks Like on Paper
* **Photographs**—Labeled Treasures; Nameless Trash
* **Recording stories**—Testing, 1-2-3: Avoiding
Technical Glitches in Interviewing
* **Research techniques**—Probate Records Share Their
Secrets

- **Societies**—The Swedish Historical Society: Tracing our Scandinavian Roots
- **Sources**—Primary Sources: Interviews, Journals, and First-Hand Accounts
- **Submitting for ordinance work**—Getting Ready for a Family Temple Day

Fashion and beauty:

- **Disappearing Acts:** Hiding Figure Flaws

Financial fitness:

- **Auctions**—Auctions with Attitude: Knowing Your Limit
- **Bargain hunting**—Discount Store Delights: Treasure Hunting in Messy Aisles
- **Coupon clipping**—Save More Than You Spend—with Coupons!
- **Children and money**—Allowance and "Family Tax": Creative Teaching about Money Matters
- **Creating a budget**—No More Godiva: Selective Splurging to Stay Happy and in the Black
- **Debt management**—Cutting the Cards: When It's Time to Eliminate Your Credit Cards
- **Estate and will planning**—Wills and Custody: What Will Happen to the Kids if We Go?
- **Estate, garage, and yard sales**—Where Will We Put It: "Bargains" You Can't Afford
- **Investment strategies**—"Who is Dow Jones and Should I Like Him?: Basic Investing Info
- **Job hunting**—Polished and Professional: The Work of Job Hunting
- **Living within your means**—Income, Outflow . . . Where Did it All Go?: Living within Your Means
- **Online shopping**—Buying Online: Shipping Fees and Other Snags
- **Planning ahead**—The Rainy Day Account: Setting Aside Consistently

- **Retirement**—Funding Freedom: Financial Security in Retirement Years
- **Taxes**—Why You Don't Really Want a Refund: Advice from a Tax Attorney
- **Tithing**—Putting Things First: What Tithing Teaches about Order and Priorities
- **Fire Safety**—Fire Chief Liu Speaks on Family Fire Escape Plans, Tuesday, Relief Society room, 7–8 P.M.

Games:

- **Board games**—Scrabble, Tuesdays, 2–4, Sister Brown's House
- **Children's games**—Where is Thumbkin?: Finger Plays, Jump Rope Chants, and Sidewalk Games
- **Magic tricks and illusions**—Quarters from Your Ears and Other Amusements
- **Juggling**—Hoopla!: Juggling Hoops for Beginners
- **Puzzles**—Crossword, Jigsaw, Sudoku, 3-D Jigsaw Puzzle Bee, Second Saturdays, 10–12 A.M., Sister Bacon's Home

Gardening:

- **Annuals**—Practical Impatiens: Planting in Shady Spots
- **Bulbs**—Protecting Bulbs from those Annoying Squirrels!
- **Community gardens**—Cultivating Community Spirit with a Public Garden
- **Desert gardens**—Blossoming as a Rose: Beautiful Desert Gardens
- **Flower gardens**—Flower Gardens: Staggered Planting for Constant Blooming
- **Herbs**—Patio Pot Herb Gardens
- **Orchards and fruit trees**—Yielding a Juicy Harvest: Tending Fruit Trees
- **Organic gardens**—Volunteers: Organic Tomatoes from Last Year's Crop

- **Perennials**—Ground Cover: Lively Variations and Lovely Shades of Green
- **Pest protection**—Deer Me: Protecting Your Garden from Wandering Deer
- **Planter ideas**—Window Boxes Made Easy
- **Rooftop gardens**—Up on the Roof: Sunshine and Soil on Top of Your Building
- **Soil types**—Deep Roots: Knowing the Best Soil to Grow In
- **Terrariums**
- **Christmas Holly and Ivy**

Health:

- **Abuse protection**—Anger Management: Couples Work Together
- **Addictions**—Al-Anon Meetings, Wednesdays, 8 P.M., United Methodist Church.
- **Anatomy**—Knee Bone's Connected to the Funny Bone: Assembling a Skeleton
- **Basic first aid**—CPR classes, Community Center, Tuesday–Thursday Nights. Call to sign up at 617–555–0001
- **Birth defects**—Coping with Spina Bifida: Support for Patients, Friends and Families
- **Bones**—Dem Dry Bones: Bone Density as Women Age
- **Breast health**—Red Hot Mama: Treating Mastitis in Nursing Mothers
- **Burns**—Three Degrees of Gory: The Varying Seriousness of Burns
- **Cancer support and survivors**—Race for the Cure! Register at 972–855–1600
- **Cardiac health**—Jazz Dance Instruction for Heart Health, Saturdays at 9 A.M.
- **Children's health issues**—Toddlers and Tubes: Ear Infections and Treatments for Youngsters
- **Colds, flu, and remedies**—Efficacious Echinacea?: Herbal Supplements that Help

- **Colon health**—It Takes Guts: What You Need to Know (but Don't Want to Talk About) Concerning Colon Health
- **"Do Not Resuscitate" and other hospital instructions**—Planning Ahead: Choosing Hospital Preferences while You're Healthy
- **Drugs**—In 1850 I Wouldn't Have Survived: The Miracle of Antibiotics
- **Eye health**—A Mote or a Beam: Protecting Your Eyes from Danger
- **Foot health**—Shoe Shopping Can Kill You: Finding Healthy and Stylish Footwear
- **Gerontology**—She Can't Remember Me: When Your Mother Gets Alzheimers
- **History of medicine**—From Pigs to People: The History of Organ Transplants
- **Hospice**—The Last Journey: Placing a Loved One in Hospice Care
- **Infertility/fertility issues**—Silent Losses; Hidden Grief: Coping with Multiple Miscarriages
- **Male health concerns**—Drag Him to the Doctor: Prostate Health and Cancer Prevention
- **Massage**—Hands-On Health: Massaging the Lower Back
- **Menstruation and menopause**—Starting and Stopping: The Biology of Menstruation and Menopause
- **Mental health: addictions, counseling, depression, eating disorders, suicide**—Rapid Cycling without a Bike: Life with Bipolar II Disorder
- **Nutrition**—Pumping Iron: Women's Special Need for Iron
- **OBGYN issues**—Cold Stirrups: What Annual Pap Smears Detect
- **Plastic surgery**—From Tattoos to Implants: Why We Do What We Do to Our Bodies
- **Poison prevention**—Keep It Down or Cough It Up?: Antidotes and Treating Poisons

+ **Prenatal health/nursing/post-partum concerns—**
Baby Blues: What's Normal and What Isn't
+ **Pulmonary health—**Hosting a 5K Lung Run: Call
1–800-ACS-2345

History:

+ **Church history—**Emma Smith and the Founding of
the Relief Society
+ **Local and community history—**Trip to the Erlander
Home Museum, Saturday, 10 A.M. Contact Sister
Holmquist
+ **World history—**Pirates of the Caribbean: The True
Stories

Home repair and improvement:

+ **Basic maintenance—**How Many Sisters Does It Take
to Screw in a Light Bulb?: Home Basics
+ **Clutter control—**Pitching a Fit: Sorting Your Stuff for
Space and Sanity
+ **Equipment—**What's in Your Toolbox: Handywoman
Must-Haves
+ **House design—**Come On In: Attractive and Practical
Entryways
+ **Interior design—**The Illusion of Space: How to Make
Tiny Rooms Seem Big
+ **Paint and paper—**Wallpapering 101: Basic Tips for
Redoing a Room
+ **Remodeling basics—**Splish Splash: Adding a Bathroom
+ **Shortcuts that work—**Duct Tape and Dry Wall:
Shortcuts from the Experts
+ **Storage Ideas—**Un-Decking the Halls: How to Store
Ornaments, Nativities, and Wreaths
+ **Tile—**Beautiful Bullnose: Easy Accents to Jazz Up
Your Bathroom

Humanitarian service:

- **International opportunities**—School Bags and Bandages: Church Humanitarian Projects
- **Local opportunities**—Fresh Starts: Creating Hygiene Kits for the Local Women's Shelter
- **National opportunities**—Katrina Aid We Can Still Offer
- **Practical tips for charitable giving**—Bang for Your Buck: How Much Actually Gets to the Charity?

International:

- **Cultures around the world**—Hmong Friends: The Hmong Community in the Twin Cities
- **Ethnic food**—The Whole Enchilada: Authentic Mexican Food
- **International current events**—Martyrs to a Cause?: Why There Are Suicide Bombers
- **Worldwide humanitarian interests**—Humanitarian Missions: Serving the Needy Worldwide

Language:

- **English as a second language**—Job Skills: Filling Out Typical Employment Applications
- **Foreign languages**—Russian ABC's: Identifying Letters in the Cyrillic Alphabet
- **Grammar and linguistics**—"Squoze" is Not a Word: Dictionaries and Our Evolving Language
- **Public speaking**—Punchy, Precise, and Polished: Making Persuasive Arguments
- **Sign language**—Deaf Pride: Understanding the Deaf Community
- **Tips for church talks**—Tips for Talks: Giving the Spirit the Best Chance Possible
- **Word games**—Balderdash/Dictionary Game Fests, third Tuesdays at Sister Booth's at 8 P.M.

Movies:

+ Hitchcock Marathon, Saturday, 6–10 P.M. at the Blake's Home. Come if you dare!

Museums:

+ Monthly Field Trips to Chicago's Museums: September 19, Shedd Aquarium

Music:

+ **Contemporary music styles**—Michael Buble and Smooth Young Jazz
+ **Classical masterpieces**—Beethoven's *Ode to Joy*— Friday, 7 P.M., University Hall on Campus
+ **Composers**—Bach to the Basics: Classical Composers for the Beginner
+ **Jazz and blues**—God Bless the Child: Billie Holliday's Life, Trials, and Talent
+ **Music around the world**—West African Rhythms: Drumming in Senegal and Gambia
+ **Music history**—American Shape Note Singing, third Wednesdays, Sister Jones's at 7 P.M.
+ **Music theory**—pp to ff: What Dynamics Do to Music

Performing arts:

+ **Instrumental performance**—Cello Recital by Sister Garcia, Saturday, 7 P.M. at the Concert Hall
+ **Choral performance**—Evanston High School Presents *Fiddler on the Roof*, April 22–25. Several of our youth are in the cast. Call 847–555–0002 for tickets.

Nature and science:

+ **Agriculture**—Acres: The Plight of the Small American Farm

- **Astronomy**—Over the Moon about New Discoveries in Space!
- **Botany**—Leaf It to Me: Identifying Poisonous Plants with Confidence
- **Chemistry**—Breathing Fire and Other Cool Stunts to Keep Your Kids Impressed
- **Camping**—Ladies' Boundary Waters Excursion July 14–18. Sign Up Today!
- **Fire prevention**—It Wasn't Just the Cow: Setting the Stage for the Great Chicago Fire
- **Environment**—Is It Hot in Here, or Is It Me?: The Myths and Realities of Global Warming
- **Geology**—Firm as the Mountains around Us: Utah Geology
- **Hikes and trails**—Hiking the Adirondacks: Great Trails of New York
- **Horticulture**—Turning Black Thumbs Green: Horticulture Basics
- **Marine life**—Whale Watching Tour, Saturday, June 9. Meet at Rockport Dock at 9 A.M.
- **Weather**—Cloud 9: Forecasting the Weather with the Clouds
- **Wildlife**—Where Have They Gone?: Endangered Animals of Our Area

Personal development:

- **Communications Skills**—Express Yourself: Communicating What You Really Mean
- **Mental Health**—Hope in the Valley: Dealing with Disappointment
- **Trust Issues**—Once Burned; Twice Shy: Developing Trust after Betrayal
- **Education**—Education after the Empty Nest
- **Goal setting**—Reaching for the Stars: Setting Motivating Goals
- **Journaling**—Life Lessons from Your Own Words
- **Leadership skills**—Servant Leadership at Work

- **Overcoming fears**—God Hath Not Given Us a Spirit of Fear: Developing Love
- **Time management**—24/7?: Remembering the Sabbath Day

Photography:

- **Cameras and how they work**—What's an F-Stop?: Getting to Know Your Camera
- **Computer programs**—Digital Magic: Exploring Photoshop
- **Digital advances**—Taking the Mystery out of Megapixels
- **Developing and printing**—Equipping Your Dark Room
- **Family portraits**—Backgrounds and Composition: Creating Beautiful Portraits
- **Studying the masters**—Ansel Adams: Master in Black and White
- **Tips for taking great photos**—Say Cheese: Tricks from Professional Photographers

Physical fitness:

- **Aerobics**—Power Walking for Aerobic Fitness
- **Badminton**—Getting into the Swing of Things: Basic Badminton
- **Bicycling**—Bike Trip to the Botanic Garden, Meet Saturday at 11 A.M. at the Church
- **Calisthenics**—Jumping Jacks and Jills: Callisthenic Exercises
- **Dance**—African Dance for Strong Quads and Gluts
- **Fencing**—En Guarde!: Pointers for Fencing
- **Gardening**—Hoe! Hoe! Hoe!: Physical Fitness through Gardening
- **Gymnastics**—Cartwheels: Keeping Nimble after Forty
- **Hiking**—Backpacks without Back Strain
- **Jogging/running**—Group Run, Mars Park, Saturday Mornings, 10 A.M. Strollers Welcome!

- **Martial arts/self-defense**—Getting a Kick Out of Life: Introduction to Karate
- **Pilates**—Strengthening the Core: Pilates Workouts for You
- **Ping-Pong**—Little Paddles; Big Fun: Playing Ping-Pong
- **Pool**—Taking the Cue: Learning to Play Pool
- **Riding**—Bareback for Beginners
- **Rock climbing**—Climbing in Rock Canyon, Saturday, 8 A.M. Bring Your Ropes and Gear
- **Rollerblading**—Rollerblading Saturday, 9 A.M. Skokie Sculpture Trail. Helmets and Pads a Must!
- **Ropes**—Learning Trust on the Ropes: Waukesha Ropes Course Instruction
- **Snow sports: Skating, skiing, sledding, snowboarding, snowman building**—Flaky Fun: Snow Angels for Grown-Ups
- **Stretching**—Head and Shoulders, Knees and Toes: Flexibility for Seniors
- **Team Sports: Basketball, bowling, golf, softball, tennis, volley ball**—Basketball Practice, Tuesday nights at 8 in the Cultural Hall
- **Walking**—Meet at Hillside Gardens, 7 A.M., two-mile circuit
- **Water Sports: Boating, surfing, swimming, waterskiing**—Ross Pool Swim, First Wednesdays, 8 P.M., weather permitting
- **Yoga**—Beyond the Downward Dog: Intermediate Yoga

Spirituality:

- **Church history**—Shall We Gather at the River: Departing Nauvoo
- **Comparative religions**—Islam and Latter-day Saints: Finding Common Ground
- **Conference talks**—Monthly Study of Recent Conference Talks at Sister Polk's Home

- **Exemplary women of faith**—Lessons from Lucy Mack Smith
- **Missionary matters**—Sharing the Gospel in Word and Deed
- **Part-member families**—Life is Good: Life in Part-Member Families
- **Prayer**—The Soul's Sincere Desire: Enriching Our Prayer Lives
- **Scripture reading**—New Creatures in Christ: Reading the Epistles of Paul
- **Service**—Hands and Hearts: Living Our Faith
- **Temple visits**—Monthly Temple Trips, Thursday mornings. Call for babysitting swaps.

Travel:

- **Day trips**—Exploring Martha's Vineyard, Saturday, August 17. Meet at the Ward Meetinghouse at 8 A.M.
- **Exotic destinations**—Tahiti: Island Paradise
- **Family vacations**—Wisconsin Dells: Even Parents Will Have Fun
- **Local treasures**—Bombay Blocks Away: Where to Buy the Best Indian Fabrics Nearby
- **Romantic getaways**—Candle Light in Colorado: Romantic Getaways near Denver
- **Planning tips**—Cruise Control: How Far in Advance Do We Have to Plan a Cruise?
- **Urban Exploration**—Around Town: Tour of Cincinnati's Public Art
- **City history**—Brattleboro in 1900: Turn of the Century Vermont
- **Fun places to discover**—Hunting for Hot Dog Stands: Compare and Contrast Night
- **Food pantries and shelters**—Monthly Shelter Dinner, St. Luke's Church. Serve at 6 P.M. on Wednesday
- **Neighborhoods**—Night on the Town: Greek Town Kabobs!

- **Local government**—Who's in Charge?: Personalities in Town Politics
- **Public transportation**—Point A to Point B: Bussing around the City
- **Security**—Thwarting Pickpockets: Simple Security Tips
- **Walking tours**—Grand Gardens of Grand Rapids: A Floral Walking Tour

Women's studies:

- **Claiming our divine heritage**—Daughters of God and Sisters of Service
- **Discovering our strengths**—Refusing Labels: Redefining Yourself as God Sees You
- **Education through the ages**—When Women Couldn't Read: Limited Worlds We No Longer Live In
- **Great women exemplars**—Jane Addams and 19th Century Social Reform for Children
- **Families throughout history**—Tracing the British Royal Lines
- **Relief Society through the years**—Bathsheba Smith's Presidency Highlights
- **Suffrage history**—Women Unite: Western Women Take a Stand for Voting Rights
- **Women in the workforce**—A Woman's Work is Never Done: Finding Balance at Home and Work

Writing:

- **Children's literature**—Picture Books and Easy Readers: What is Your Child Ready For?
- **Getting published**—What is a Query Letter and How Do You Write One?
- **Journalism**—Networking with the Local Press
- **Magazine pieces**—Pitching Pieces to the Right Places
- **Manuscript critique groups**—Constructive Criticism from Writing Peers

- **Memoir and journals**—Capturing Moments and Memories with the Written Word
- **Novels**—Truth Told in Literature: Discovering Great Novels
- **Opinion pieces**—Supporting Your Position: Writing Opinions for Newspapers
- **Poetry**—Haiku. Can You?: Poetry in Three Lines and Seventeen Syllables
- **Short stories**—Beginnings, Middles, and Ends: Crafting Great Short Stories
- **Travel writing**—Turn our Trip into Money: Marketing Your Travel Writing

X-ray and radiation advances:

- The Miracle of MRIs

Young at heart and staying that way:

- Seniors Stand Up Comedy, First Fridays at 7 P.M. in the Cultural Hall

Yuletide planning:

- Community Nativity Displays at the Stake Center, December 1–20. All Welcome.

Zoos

- Mom and Tot Zoo Day, Saturday, May 20. Meet at the Zoo Entrance at 10 A.M.

A-Z by Welfare Wheel Topics

When planning enrichment events and activities, many wards use the church handbook welfare wheel topics as a valuable guide for planning.

Church Handbook Welfare Wheel:

* Literacy and Education
* Career Development
* Financial and Resource Management
* Home Production and Storage
* Physical Health
* Social, Emotional, and Spiritual Strength

The following pages show the "A–Z with Curves" from the previous section loosely categorized by the topics on the Welfare Wheel. Because the topics are extremely broad, there is inevitable overlap. Should beading be considered in the category of "Emotional Health" because it's so much fun? Or should it be in the "Literacy and Education" component because it may be something the sisters are learning for the first time? Or is this a skill that could be developed into a career for the right person? It could be in each! As you begin your own sorting and sifting of ideas, find a pattern that works for you and have fun with it.

Literacy and education:

- The ABC's of Helping Children Read
- Acres: The Plight of the Small American Farm
- Afraid of the Dark?: Getting Deep Tones in Your Black and White Pencil Work
- Agatha Christie and the Miss Marple Mysteries
- Ansel Adams: Master in Black and White
- Around the Globe: Exploring Shakespeare's Globe Theater
- Awl or Nothing?: Becoming Familiar with Woodworking Tools
- Bach to the Basics: Classical Composers for the Beginner
- Bead-decked and Bead-dazzled: Beading for Beginners
- Beginnings, Middles, and Ends: Crafting Great Short Stories
- Boston's Big Dig: Modern Archeological Discoveries
- Brattleboro in 1900: Turn of the Century Vermont
- Brush Up on Painting: Selecting the Correct Tools for Your Medium
- Capturing Moments and Memories with the Written Word
- The Charles Dawes House: Welcome to the Evanston Historical Society
- Cloud 9: Forecasting the Weather with the Clouds
- Coyotes on Broadway?: Animal Predators in Urban Areas

- Cut, Paste, Create!: Creating Art with All Kinds of Stuff
- Denzel Washington: A Man to Watch
- Digital Magic: Exploring PhotoShop
- Disappearing Acts: Hiding Figure Flaws
- Education after the Empty Nest
- Eleanor Roosevelt: Her Life and Times
- Equipping Your Dark Room
- Explosion of Styles: Caldecott Award Winners of the last Fifty Years
- Eye Smarts: Designing a Pleasing Composition
- Firm as the Mountains Around Us: Utah Geology
- Flannery O'Connor and Literature of the South
- Fun with Fimo: Working with Polymer Clay
- Giggle, Gaggle, Google!: Searching on the Internet
- Global Positioning System: A Wife's Best Friend
- God Bless the Child: Billie Holliday's Life, Trials, and Talent
- Hooray for Spell Check!: Word Processing Wonders
- Haiku. Can You?: Poetry in Three Lines and Seventeen Syllables
- Handle with Care: The Complex World of the Internet
- He's No Coward: Noel Coward's Comedies
- Hiking the Adirondacks: Great Trails of New York
- Horses for the Hapsburgs: The History of the Elegant Lipizzan Stallions
- Is It Hot in Here, or Is It Me?: The Myths and Realities of Global Warming
- It Wasn't Just the Cow: Setting the Stage for the Great Chicago Fire
- Jan Vermeer: Master in the Dutch Golden Age
- Jane Addams and 19th Century Social Reform for Children
- Line upon Line Works for Computers, Too!
- Long-Stemmed and Lovely: Arranging Roses
- Mainstreaming or Special Education: What's the Best for My Child?
- Make it Pop: Using Color Theory to Your Advantage

- Martyrs to a Cause?: Why There Are Suicide Bombers
- Mazda or Model T?: Differences between Car Makes and Models
- Michael Buble and Smooth Young Jazz
- My Child the Nerd: Socializing Brilliant Children
- Not Too Young to Dye: Tie-dying Socks and T-shirts
- Over the Moon about New Discoveries in Space!
- Picture Books and Easy Readers: What is Your Child Ready For?
- Picture Book Favorites: Story Time for Moms and Tots
- Pint-Sized Pets: Hamsters, Gerbils, and Mice
- Pirates of the Caribbean: The True Stories
- Pouring Paper: Basics of Handmade Papermaking
- Powders and Paints: Basic Equipment for Rubber Stamping
- pp to ff: What Dynamics Do to Music
- Public, Private, or at Home?: Pluses and Minuses of Each Kind of Schooling
- Punchy, Precise, and Polished: Making Persuasive Arguments
- Pythons on Parade!: Snakes and Constrictors as Pets
- Rah! Rah! Rumble Seats!: Antique Cars and Horseless Carriages
- Retrieving Your Digital Photos
- Russian ABC's: Identifying Letters in the Cyrillic Alphabet
- Scented Candles for Christmas
- The Scottish Play: Macbeth and Its Lore
- Spinsters Unite!: Learning to use a Spinning Wheel
- "Squoze" is Not a Word: Dictionaries and Our Evolving Language
- Storing These Treasures: Where to Put My Scrapbooks When I'm Done
- Sturm und Drang: 18th Century German Literature
- Tahiti: Island Paradise
- Taking the Cue: Learning to Play Pool
- Taking the Mystery out of Megapixels

- Tole Painting: Learning the Crafts of our Scandinavian Ancestors
- Tracing the British Royal Lines
- Transforming that Tabletop: Decoupage for Furniture
- A Trip Around the World: Coins of Many Countries
- Truth Told in Literature: Discovering Great Novels
- Warp, Woof, and Wool: Setting Up a Navajo Loom
- Wax On, Wax Off: Fabric Art with Batik
- West African Rhythms: Drumming in Senegal and Gambia
- What's an F-Stop?: Getting to Know Your Camera
- When Women Couldn't Read: Limited Worlds We No Longer Live In
- Where Have They Gone?: Endangered Animals of Our Area
- Who's in Charge?: Personalities in Town Politics
- Wide Enough to Turn a Team: Brigham Young's Salt Lake City
- Wildlife in Our Area
- Winged and Wading Wonders: Identifying Flamingos, Herons, and Cranes
- Wisconsin Dells: Even Parents Will Have Fun

Career development:

- Backgrounds and Composition: Creating Professional Photographic Portraits
- Beaded, Beautiful Bling!: Beaded Jewelry You Could Sell
- Being an Effective Boss
- Beyond the Suggestion Box: Expressing Your Job Concerns Persuasively
- CEO, IPO, M-O-U-S-E: Learning "Compan-ese"
- Chips and Chunks of China: Creating Mosaic Works of Art
- Download and Delete: Basic Jargon to Know
- Express Yourself: Communicating What You Really Mean

- Getting Published: What is a Query Letter and How Do You Write One?
- Going Down: Coal Mine Strikes and Safety
- Gospel Principles of Leadership that Apply in the Workplace
- An Honest Day's Wage: Being an Effective Employee
- In a Bind: Comb, Coil, and Wiring Book-Binding Techniques
- Job Skills: Filling Out Typical Employment Applications
- Journalism: Networking with the Local Press
- Manuscript Critique Groups: Constructive Criticism from Writing Peers
- Megabytes and Major Bucks: Computer Systems and Setups
- The Mouse Race: Keeping Your Computer Skills Up to Date
- A New Leash on Life: Starting Your Own Dog-Walking Service
- Pitching Magazine Pieces to the Right Places
- Polished and Professional: The Work of Job Hunting
- Portraits that Come Alive: Shadows and Planes
- Reaching for the Stars: Setting Motivating Goals
- Research and Eye Contact: Landing the Job through the Interview
- Résumé Writing: Job Skills Learned through Church Callings
- The Revolving Door: Creating Time to be Together
- Safe and Secure: Selecting On-Site Childcare
- Say Cheese: Tricks from Professional Photographers
- Servant Leadership at Work
- Stained Glass Color and Texture: Selecting Which Glass to Use
- Supporting Your Position: Writing Opinions for Newspapers
- Throwing Yourself into It: Potter's Wheel Basics
- Tooling Leather Like a Pro

- Turn our Trip into Money: Marketing Your Travel Writing
- What Do These Buttons Do?: Bonding with Your Cell Phone
- What to Do When You Have a Boss from Heck
- What's Covered?: Understanding your Benefits Package
- Working with Silver: The Technique of Lost Wax Casting
- Worth Every Penny: How to Ask for a Raise

Financial and resource management:

- Allowance and "Family Tax": Creative Teaching about Money Matters
- Auctions with Attitude: Knowing Your Limit
- Bang for Your Buck: How Much Actually Gets to the Charity
- Biodiesel and Hybrid Cars: Vehicles of the Future . . . or the Present?
- Brittle Bundles: Preserving Our Heirlooms
- Buying Online: Shipping Fees and Other Snags
- Community Conservation Efforts
- Cutting the Cards: When It's Time to Eliminate Your Credit Cards
- Discount Store Delights: Treasure Hunting in Messy Aisles
- Funding Freedom: Financial Security in Retirement Years
- Gems among the Junk: Finding Antiques at Garage and Estate Sales
- How Much is a Tooth Worth?: Teaching Children about Money and Molars
- Income, Outflow . . . Where Did It All Go?: Living within Your Means
- Let the Sun Shine: Practical Solar Panels
- The Middle East and the Economics of Oil

- No More Godiva: Selective Splurging to Stay Happy and in the Black
- Paper or Plastic?: A Bigger Question Than You Think
- Point A to Point B: Bussing around the City
- Putting Things First: What Tithing Teaches about Order and Priorities
- The Rainy Day Account: Setting Aside Consistently
- Road Shows without Rehearsals: Appraising our Antiques
- Save More Than You Spend—with Coupons!
- Spud Spectacular: Potato Print Gift Wrap and Greeting Cards
- Standards Night: Learning to Drive Stick Shift in the Ward Meetinghouse Parking Lot
- Tran$mi$$ion Problems to Watch Out For
- Turnaround Trees: Natural and Artificial Reforestation
- Warm and Friendly: Environmentally Sound and Effective Home Insulation
- Water Rights and Our State Laws
- Where Will We Put It: "Bargains" You Can't Afford
- "Who is Dow Jones and Should I Like Him?: Basic Investing Info
- Wills and Custody: What Will Happen to the Kids if We Go?
- Why You Don't Really Want a Refund: Advice from a Tax Attorney

Home production and storage:

- Appealing Apricots: Recipes Sure to Please
- Basil and Balsamic: Easy Dipping Recipes to Try
- Beautiful Bullnose: Easy Accents to Jazz Up Your Bathroom
- Beyond Beans: Getting Enough Protein in Tasty Ways
- Blossoming as a Rose: Beautiful Desert Gardens
- Bombay Blocks Away: Where to Buy the Best Indian Fabrics Nearby

- Cabins to Mansions: Early Styles in American Architecture
- Christmas Holly and Ivy Terrariums
- Clam Up: New England and Manhattan Clam Chowders
- Clementines: Where Do These Tasty Citrus Fruits Come From?
- Come On In: Attractive and Practical Entryways
- Compost and Conservation: What You Can Do
- Cultivating Community Spirit with a Public Garden
- Deep Roots: Knowing the Best Soil to Grow In
- Deer Me: Protecting Your Garden from Wandering Deer
- Duct Tape and Dry Wall: Short Cuts from the Experts
- Dutch Oven Delights!
- Elegant Entertaining from Linens to Lamb Chops
- Eye on Rye: Baking Rolls and Breads with Rye
- Five-Star Ramen Noodles Recipes
- Flower Gardens: Staggered Planting for Constant Blooming
- Great Grilled Vegetables!
- Ground Cover: Lively Variations and Lovely Shades of Green
- How Long Will This Keep?: Freezing Food Basics
- How Many Sisters Does it Take to Screw in a Light Bulb?: Home Basics
- If It Walks Like a Duck: Care and Feeding of Domestic Fowl
- The Illusion of Space: How to Make Tiny Rooms Seem Big
- Jewels in Jars: Canning Basics
- Keep a Lid on It: Secrets to Blender Success
- Lemon Meringue Cake: A Mix Mystery Special
- Lotsa Lasagna: Italian Food for the Whole Huge Family
- Making Meats Tender and Savory with Marinades
- Measuring Spoons and Mixing Bowls: Standard Supplies for your Kitchen

- Nostalgia: Hot Breakfasts Like Grandma Made
- Nothin' Says Lovin': Visiting Teaching Treats from the Oven
- Outrageously Good Orzo
- Patio Pot Herb Gardens
- Patio Tomatoes that Taste Terrific
- Pie-o-My-o-My!
- Pitching a Fit: Sorting Your Stuff for Space and Sanity
- Plant a Garden; Grow a Village
- Practical Impatiens: Planting in Shady Spots
- The Problem of Pests: Solutions in Organic Gardening
- Protecting Bulbs from Those Annoying Squirrels!
- Quillows: Part Quilt, Part Pillow—All Fun!
- Ranch, Prairie, or Victorian: What Style Is Your House?
- Slow Cooking Sweetness: Puddings and Desserts in the Crock Pot
- Splish Splash: Adding a Bathroom
- Stovetop Cooking: Tasty One-Dish Meals
- Turning Black Thumbs Green: Horticulture Basics
- Un-Decking the Halls: How to Store Ornaments, Nativities, and Wreaths
- Up on the Roof: Sunshine and Soil on top of Your Building
- Volunteers: Organic Tomatoes from Last Year's Crop
- Wallpapering 101: Basic Tips for Redoing a Room
- What Cut is What?: Studying the Butcher's Chart
- What's in Your Toolbox: Handywoman Must-Haves
- What's the Difference: Basics of Convection Oven Cooking
- Which Way Does the Knife Edge Point?: Basic Table Settings
- The Whole Enchilada: Authentic Mexican Food
- Window Boxes Made Easy
- Yielding a Juicy Harvest: Tending Fruit Trees
- The Yolks on You!: Egg White Creations

Physical health:

- African Dance for Strong Quads and Gluts
- Baby Basics: What to Expect during Your First Week at Home
- Baby Blues: What's Normal and What Isn't?
- Backpacks without Back Strain
- Bareback for Beginners
- Beyond the Downward Dog: Intermediate Yoga
- Cancer support and survivors: Race for the Cure! Register at 972–855–1600
- Cartwheels: Keeping Nimble after Forty
- Cell Phones and Highway Safety
- Cold Stirrups: What Annual Pap Smears Detect
- Comfort Kits for Chemotherapy
- Coping with Spina Bifida: Support for Patients, Friends, and Families
- CPR classes, Community Center, Tuesday–Thursday Nights. Call to sign up at 617–555–0001.
- Dem Dry Bones: Bone Density as Women Age
- "Do Not Resuscitate": Choosing Hospital Preferences while You're Healthy
- Dogs for the Deaf: Training Service Animals for the Hearing Impaired
- Drag Him to the Doctor: Prostate Health and Cancer Prevention
- Efficacious Echinacea?: Herbal Supplements That Help Colds and Flu
- En Guarde!: Pointers for Fencing
- Fire Chief Liu Speaks on Family Fire Escape Plans, Tuesday, Relief Society room, 7–8 P.M.
- From Pigs to People: The History of Organ Transplants
- From Tattoos to Implants: Why We Do What We Do to Our Bodies
- Getting a Kick Out of Life: Introduction to Karate
- Getting into the Swing of Things: Basic Badminton

- A Gluten-Free Life Made Easier
- Hands on Health: Massaging the Lower Back
- Head and Shoulders, Knees and Toes: Flexibility for Seniors
- Hoe! Hoe! Hoe!: Physical Fitness through Gardening
- Hosting a 5K Lung Run: Call 1–800-ACS-2345
- In 1850 I Wouldn't Have Survived: The Miracle of Antibiotics
- It Takes Guts: What You Need to Know but Don't Want to Ask About Colon Health
- Jazz Dance Instruction for Heart Health, Saturdays at 9 A.M.
- Jumping Jacks and Jills: Callisthenic Exercises
- Just a Fat Cat?: Distinguishing Symptoms That Need a Vet's Attention
- Keep it Down or Cough it Up?: Antidotes and Treating Poisons
- Knee Bone's Connected to the Funny Bone: Assembling a Skeleton
- The Last Journey: Placing a Loved One in Hospice Care
- Leaf It to Me: Identifying Poisonous Plants with Confidence
- Little Paddles; Big Fun: Playing Ping-Pong
- Managing Migraines
- The Miracle of MRIs
- A Mote or a Beam: Protecting Your Eyes from Danger
- Power Walking for Aerobic Fitness
- Pregnancy Month by Month: Valuable Information for First-Time Moms
- Pumping Iron: Women's Special Need for Iron
- Rapid Cycling without a Bike: Life with Bipolar II Disorder
- Red Hot Mama: Treating Mastitis in Nursing Mothers
- Three Degrees of Gory: The Varying Seriousness of Burns
- She Can't Remember Me: When Your Mother Gets Alzheimer's

- Shoe Shopping Can Kill You: Finding Healthy and Stylish Footwear
- Silent Losses; Hidden Grief: Coping with Multiple Miscarriages
- Some Are Fancy on the Outside: Body Awareness for Toddlers
- Starting and Stopping: The Biology of Menstruation and Menopause
- Strengthening the Core: Pilates Workouts for You
- Toddlers and Tubes: Ear Infections and Treatments for Youngsters
- Young at Heart and Staying that Way

Social, emotional, and spiritual strength:

- American Shape Note Singing, Third Wednesdays, Sister Jones's at 7 P.M.
- Anger Management: Couples Work Together
- Around Town: Tour of Cincinnati's Public Art
- Backstage Tour at the Regency Theater, June 22, 4 P.M.
- Balderdash/Dictionary Game Fests, Third Tuesdays at Sister Booth's at 8 P.M.
- Basketball Practice, Tuesday nights at 8 P.M. in the Cultural Hall
- Bathsheba Smith's Presidency Highlights
- Becoming a Citizen: How to Start
- Beethoven's Ode to Joy—Friday, 7 P.M., University Hall on Campus
- Bike Trip to the Botanic Garden, Meet Saturday at 11 A.M. at the Church
- Boys are Stupid; Girls are Gross: Are My Children Sexist?
- Breathing Fire and Other Cool Stunts to Keep Your Kids Impressed
- Candlelight in Colorado: Romantic Getaways near Denver
- Care Packages for Your Serving Sons and Daughters

- Cello Recital by Sister Garcia, Saturday, 7 P.M. at the Concert Hall.
- Climbing in Rock Canyon, Saturday, 8 A.M. Bring Your Ropes and Gear
- Clues from the Obits: Discovering Ancestors in Odd Ways
- Community Nativity Displays at the stake Center, December 1–20. All Welcome.
- Cruise Control: How Far in Advance Do We Have to Plan a Cruise?
- Daughters of God and Sisters of Service
- Deaf Pride: Understanding the Deaf Community
- Disaster Aid We Can Still Offer
- Elgin High School Presents *West Side Story*, April 22–25
- Emma Smith and the Founding of the Relief Society
- Exploring Martha's Vineyard, Saturday, August 17. Meet at the Ward Meetinghouse at 8 A.M.
- Family Photographs: Labeled Treasures; Nameless Trash
- Fiddler on the Spoof: Creating Our Own Musical
- Field Trip to the Family History Library, Saturday, July 6, 10–12 A.M.
- Flaky Fun this Friday: Snow Angels for Grown-Ups. Hot Chocolate Included!
- For Every Bed a Blanket: Helping the Homeless Shelters
- Fresh Starts: Creating Hygiene Kits for the Local Women's Shelter
- Field Trips Monthly to Chicago's Museums: September 19, Shedd Aquarium
- The Gains and Strains of Family Reunions
- Getting Ready for a Family Temple Day
- Girls' Night Out: Monthly Dinners at Downtown Restaurants
- God Hath Not Given Us a Spirit of Fear: Developing Love and Conquering Fear

- Grand Gardens of Grand Rapids: A Floral Walking Tour
- Gross Motor Gatherings—Ackerman Park, Wednesdays at 9 A.M.
- Group Run, Mars Park, Saturday Mornings, 10 A.M. Strollers Welcome!
- Hands and Hearts: Living Our Faith
- Help! My Angel Has Turned into a Devil!
- Hitchcock Marathon, Saturday, 6–10 P.M. at the Blake's Home. Come if you dare!
- Hmong Friends: The Hmong Community in the Twin Cities
- Hoopla!: Juggling Hoops for Beginners
- Hope in the Valley: Dealing with disappointment
- Humanitarian Missions: Serving the Needy Worldwide
- Hunting for Hot Dog Stands: Compare and Contrast Night
- Islam and Latter-day Saints: Finding Common Ground
- Jigsaw Puzzle Bee, Second Saturdays, 10–12 A.M., Sister Bacon's Home
- Journaling: Life Lessons from Your Own Words
- Keeping Kids Active after School
- Keeping Us in Stitches: Weekly Gatherings to Visit and Do Handwork
- Ladies' Boundary Waters Excursion July 14–18. Sign Up Today!
- Ladling Love: Soup Kitchen Volunteer Experiences in Our Town
- Learning Trust on the Ropes: Waukesha Ropes Course Instruction
- Lessons from Lucy Mack Smith
- Life Is Good: Life in Part-Member Families
- Line upon Line: What Twelve Generations Looks Like on Paper
- The Lost Art of Thank You Notes
- Meet at Hillside Gardens, 7 A.M., two-mile walking circuit

- Mom and Tot Zoo Day, Saturday, May 20. Meet at Zoo Entrance at 10 A.M.
- Monthly Study of recent Conference Talks at Sister Polk's Home
- Monthly Temple Trips, Thursday mornings. Call for babysitting swaps.
- New Creatures in Christ: Reading the Epistles of Paul
- Night on the Town: Greek Town Kabobs!
- No Ponies Needed: Simple Birthday Parties with Less Stress
- Once Burned; Twice Shy: Developing Trust after Betrayal
- Pioneer Journals: A Reader's Theater May 1, 7–8 P.M., Cultural Hall
- Pool Swim, First Wednesdays, 8 P.M., Weather Permitting
- Pop-Up Greeting Cards You Can Make at Home
- Primary Sources: Interviews, Journals, and First-Hand Accounts
- Probate Records Share Their Secrets
- Quarters From Your Ears and Other Amusements
- Refusing Labels: Redefining Yourself as God Sees You
- Rollerblading Saturday, 9 A.M. Skokie Sculpture Trail. Helmets and Pads a Must!
- The Sacred in the Shoe Box: How I Met My Ancestors
- School Bags and Bandages: Church Humanitarian Projects
- Scrabble, Tuesdays, 2–4 P.M., Sister Brown's House
- Seniors Stand-Up Comedy, First Fridays at 7 P.M. in the Cultural Hall
- Shall We Gather at the River: Departing Nauvoo
- Sharing the Gospel in Word and Deed
- Short, Sweets, and to the Point: Strategies for Successful Family Nights
- Side-Splitting Sisters Improv Group—Monthly, First Saturdays, 7–9 P.M.
- Single Moms: Carving out Time for Yourself

- Sleep Deprivation and Early Morning Seminary: Facts and Strategies
- Snapdragons and Seniors: Planting Flowers at the Senior Center
- The Soul's Sincere Desire: Enriching Our Prayer Lives
- Spoil Them and Send them Home?: Connecting with Your Grandchildren
- Struggling in the Middle: Caring for Parents as well as Children
- The Swedish Historical Society: Tracing Our Scandinavian Roots
- Testing, 1–2–3: Avoiding Technical Glitches in Interviewing
- Thanksgiving Cornucopia Ideas to Be Thankful For
- Thwarting Pickpockets: Simple Security Tips
- Tips for Talks: Giving the Spirit the Best Chance Possible
- Trip to the Erlander Home Museum, Saturday, 10 A.M. Contact Sister Holmquist
- 24/7?: Remembering the Sabbath Day to Keep it Holy
- Valentine's Brunch, February 14, from 11 A.M. to 1 P.M. at Sister Smoot's
- A Visit to the Lion House, Saturday, October 10. Meet there at 10 A.M.
- Whale Watching Tour, Saturday, June 9. Meet at Rockport Dock at 9 A.M.
- Where is Thumbkin?: Finger Plays, Jump Rope Chants, and Sidewalk Games
- Whose Name Goes Where on a Family Group Sheet?
- A Woman's Work Is Never Done: Finding Balance at Home and Work
- Women Unite: Western Women Take a Stand for Voting Rights
- Writing Our Own: Writing and Producing One Acts—a Three-Month Adventure
- Yes and No: Questions to Get Them Talking

A-Z Potpourri

Here is a completely new batch of titles for your enrichment and amusement. They are in alphabetical order but not in any thematic order. This is just a free-wheeling, anything-goes array of ideas for good activities. These titles could be for one-occasion events or as part of a longer series or interest group. Some of them might simply remind you of a personal interest you want to pursue. Others will just leave you scratching you head and wondering why anyone would be interested in *that!*

- ◆ Aardvarks to Zebras: A Trip to the Zoo
- ◆ ABC's of Literacy: Teaching a Love of Reading
- ◆ Accountability: Teaching Values to Our Children
- ◆ Achoo! Achoo!: Hay Fever and Allergies
- ◆ Adventures with Autism: A Day on the Home Front
- ◆ African-American Heroes and Heroines
- ◆ African Harvest: The Growth of the Church in Africa
- ◆ After a Divorce: Living a Whole, Healthy, and Happy Life
- ◆ After the Flood: Lessons from Katrina
- ◆ Alaska: Land of Wilderness and Warm Hearts
- ◆ All Dressed Up and Somewhere to Go!: A Night on the Town in (your city or area)
- ◆ All the Bells and Whistles: An Introduction to Auxiliary Percussion Instruments
- ◆ Alzheimer's Realities
- ◆ Amazing: The Miracle of Grace
- ◆ Anxious to Please and Other Self-defeating Tendencies: Women's Emotional Health
- ◆ Appalachian Trail Mix: Stories, Lore, and Life in Appalachia
- ◆ Aunt-cestors: Genealogy on Collateral Lines

- Backpacks on Board: Traveling with Children
- Bang for Your Buck: Smart Shopping Tips
- Barbecue Babes and Grillin' Gals
- Barbie to Condoleeza: Finding Healthy Role Models for Our Daughters
- Because I Said So: Pitfalls in Parenting
- Beautiful, Abundant Bananas
- Becoming Our Mothers: How to Avoid or Embrace the Possibility
- Being and Becoming: Finding Fulfillment in Life
- Beyond the Empty Nest: Transitions Can Be Fun
- Beyond the Veil: Uplifting True Stories of Help and Consolation
- Blackout: Are You Prepared if the Lights Go Out?
- Blended Families: Mix, Pulse, or Puree?
- Books We Love
- Borrowing Trouble: Some Common Financial Goof-ups
- Breakout Session: Dermatology and You
- Breathing Basics: There's More to It than You Think
- Building the Kingdom: Challenges and Opportunities in Our Modern World
- Bulk Buying Do's and Don'ts
- Bushel and a Peck: We Love Apples!

- Can You Dig It?: Gardening Basics
- Campfire Cuisine: Cooking in the Great Outdoors
- Care and Feeding of a Curmudgeon: How to Live Happily with a Grump
- Cash-Flow Crisis: Averting Financial Disasters
- Ceilings Are Not Eternal: Patching and Plastering Tips for What's Overhead
- Charity Begins at Home: Service Projects You Can Do in Your Spare Time
- Cheap Dates: Fun Things to Do for Not Much Money
- Cheese It: Navigating Your Whey around the Cheeses of the World
- Children in Crisis: Poverty in America
- Chocolate Challenge: A Competitive Chocolate Bake-Off
- Clever Christmas Card Ideas
- Closets Without Clutter
- Cold Cut Cravings: Sandwich Ideas You'll Love to Make and Eat
- Contracts and Clauses: A Lawyer Helps Us Know What We're Signing
- Covenant People: Exploring the Promises We Make and Keep
- Creepy Crawlers: More than You Ever Wanted to Know about Bugs
- Crime Busters: Careers in Law Enforcement
- Critters to the Rescue: Great Stories of Heroic Animals
- Crock-Pot Magic
- Culture Clashes on the Home Front: Trouble Shooting in Marriage

- Daily Planners: Creating a Routine That Works for You
- Daily Regimens for Spiritual, Physical, and Emotional Health
- Dear Sir or Madam: Business Correspondence in a New Era
- Decorating on a Dime: How to Spruce up a Room when Time and Money Are Short
- Deep-Fried Delights: Doughnuts and Other Wickedly Good Treats
- Deliberations: When Jury Duty Calls
- Diapers to Diamonds: Raising Girls in a Prestige-Driven Society
- Disaster Preparedness 101
- Dishing it Out: Creating Large Group Meals
- Divine Potential: Coming to Know God's Perspective of Our Lives
- Domestic Abuse: Symptoms, Support, and the Legal System
- Don't Even Think about It: Developing Personal Boundaries and Making Them Work
- The Dope on Dope: The Drug Crisis in America and Its Impact Locally
- Do-Re-Mi: Vocal Tips for Singers Who Can Only Go So-Fa
- Do-Si-Do: Square Dances and Reels
- Drowsy Driving: Danger on the Road
- Dying to be Thin: Figures and Facts about Anorexia and Eating Disorders

- Eagles, Hawks, and Vultures: Raptors of the World
- Easter Traditions around the World
- The Economics of Poverty: Understanding Causes and Developing Solutions
- Egg-cellent Egg-stravaganza: Recipes that Will Crack You Up
- Eggplants and Artichokes: Great Recipes with Eccentric Vegetables
- Elegant Entertaining on a Shoestring
- Elementary, My Dear Watson!: Sherlock Holmes Mysteries
- Eliza R. Snow: President, Poet, and Pioneer
- Empty Bowl Project: Feeding the Hungry in Our Community
- Endowed with Power from on High: Making the Most of Our Temple Covenants
- Engaged in Good Causes: Local, National, and Worldwide Humanitarian Service
- Enter at Your Own Risk: Household Hazards You Can Avoid
- Everybody's a Critic: Dealing with Negativity
- Eureka!: Cool Discoveries of the Past Fifty Years
- Euros, Dollars, and International Investing
- Examples of Faith: Modern Women We Can Learn From
- Extra! Extra! Read All About It!: Journalism in Today's World
- Exotic Animals of Africa from Addax to Zebu
- Extreme Sports: Oddball Things People Do for Fun

- The Fabulous Juggling Women: Keeping Balance in our Busy Lives
- Fancy Footwork: Ballroom Dancing for Beginners
- Families, Feuds, and Forgiveness: Facing Tough Realities of Family Life
- Famine Relief: Effective Help from a Distance
- Fascinating Fiction of the 21st Century
- Faux or Real: Pearls of Various Prices
- Feasts: Culinary Celebrations around the World
- Feathers, Fabric, and Fibers: Creative Cloth Art
- Finding Our Way: Navigating Our Public Transportation System
- Finger Paints and Sidewalk Chalk: Nurturing Your Child's Creativity
- Fingerprints and DNA: The Real Science behind CSI
- Fit for a Crown of Gold: Dental Technology in the 21st Century
- Fit to be Tied: Fun Ideas in Bow Making
- Flab Be Gone: Fitness and Toning for All Body Types
- Flexibility and Fitness: Stretching and Bending to Keep You on the Move
- The Flush of Success: Toilet Training in the 21st Century
- Flying Fingers: Advanced Crocheting and Knitting
- Fly Fishing: The Al-Lure of a Tranquil Sport
- Food Fights and Midnight Howls: Creating Fond Family Traditions
- For Crying Out Loud: The Therapeutic Benefits of Tears and Laughter
- Friends Forever: Keeping in Touch in a Busy World

- From Advent to Easter: Familiarizing Ourselves with the Calendar of other Christians
- Fun with Forks: Fondues for all Occasions
- Fur's a-Flyin': Traveling with Pets

- Genes and Accountability: How Our Bodies Effect Our Behavior
- Getting the Lead Out: Eliminating Housing Hazards
- Getting the Lead Out: Pencil Sketching in the Great Outdoors
- Getting Trunky: Jumper Cables, a Spare Tire, and Other Car Trunk Essentials
- Gimme! Gimme!: Teaching and Developing Impulse Control
- Girls Just Wanna Have Fun: Creative Ideas for Good Times with Your Girlfriends
- Global Warming: Facts, Fiction, and Things We Can Do Something About
- Good Grief: Healing After a Major Loss
- Good Lookin': Lenses, Lasik, and Eye Health
- Goosing the Muse: Exercises to Enliven Your Imagination (Your Art, Writing, and Music)
- Gorgeous Gorges: Scenic Wonders of America
- Grains: What Quinoa, Barley, and Spelt Can Do for You
- Grandma, MorMor, Nana, and Oma: The Joy of Being a Grandmother
- Grapes, Berries, and Other Sweet, Round Goodies
- The Grass is Always Greener: Being Content with What We Have
- The Grass Is Always Greener: Environmentally Friendly Yard and Lawn Care
- Great Dames: Important Women of the 21st Century (17th, 18th, 19th, or 20th)

- Great Expectations: Pre-Natal Care for First-Time Moms
- Green Is Not Just a Color: Environmental Habits You Can Develop
- Guzzle No More: Gas, Oil, and Renewable Resources

- Hand Me That Hammer, Hubby: Taking Home Repair into Our Own Hands
- Happiness and Heartache: Some Realities of Motherhood
- Haven't Been There; Haven't Done That: New and Exciting Vacation Ideas
- Having the Courage of Our Convictions
- Having Our Say: Claiming Our Voices
- Heart Art: Cards, Crafts, and Poetry for Valentine's Day
- The Heartbreak of Infertility
- Herb Gardens for Fun, Food, and Profit
- He Said; She Said: Learning How Men and Women Communicate Differently
- Ho Ho Ho?: Stress Reduction During the Holidays
- Holiday Handcrafts for the Glue-gun Impaired
- Holiday Handcrafts for the Seriously Crafty
- Holiday Handcrafts in a Snap, on a Budget, and Sure to Please
- The Holy Ghost: Pondering the Power of This Member of the Godhead
- Hosannas and Handkerchiefs: Remembering our Temple's Dedication
- Hot Stuff!: Cooking with Chilies, Peppers, and Hot Sauces
- Hula, Moolah, and Hotels: Planning Your Hawaiian Holiday
- Hunger at Home and around the World: How We Can Help
- Husbands, Fathers, Brothers, Sons: Understanding the Men in Our Lives
- Huzzah!: Life (Art, Literature, Games, or Music) in the Renaissance

- I Don't Know What to Say: Learning to Mourn with Those Who Mourn
- "I Love You. Go Away": Destructive Messages We May Be Sending or Receiving
- I Never Promised You a Rose Garden . . . but Here's How to Tend One
- I Want, You Want, We Want: Setting Personal and Family Goals
- If Only: Identifying and Confronting Stumbling Blocks to Our Happiness
- If You Give a Mouse a Cookie: Teaching Consequences to Our Children
- Incentives That Work: Beating Procrastination
- Incentives That Work: Getting Your Kids to Help around the House
- Interpretive Dance: The Aesthetic and Therapeutic Pleasures of Movement

- Inheriting: What to Do with the Windfall from Aunt Sadie's Will
- Inspiration Daily: Creating Your Own Book of Uplifting Scriptures and Quotes
- Instilling Peace: Regular Regimens That Will Nourish our Spirits
- Invitations: From Traditional to Funky and Every Kind In-between
- International Cuisine Fest
- Investing: Planning for a Secure Future in a Speculative Field
- Ipods, MP3s and the New Plugged-In World
- Iroquois, Sioux, and Cherokee: Tribes of Native Americans
- It's in the Bag: Gift Bags for All Occasions

- Jack-o-Lanterns and Painted Gourds: Hands-On Halloween Decorations
- Jacks, Jump Rope, and Marbles: Tried and True Games for Children
- Jams, Jellies, and Other Gems in Jars
- Jeepers Creepers: Trellises, Ivies, and Other Climbing Plants
- Jell-O!: Retro Recipes for a Fond, Familiar Food
- The Jerusalem Center: The Plan, Programs, and Purpose of BYU Jerusalem Center
- Jerusalem—Past and Present
- *Jesus the Christ*: A Relief Society Study of Talmage's Book about the Savior
- Jewish Feasts and Holidays and Connections with the Restored Gospel
- Jewish Literature through the Ages
- Jingle Bells: Sleigh Rides, Snow Picnics, and Other Fun Winter Entertainments
- Judge Not—but Use Judgment: Learning from Our Bad Experiences
- Juggling: The Fine Art of Tossing Things from Beanbags to Bowling Pins
- Jubilant Faith: Making Your Spiritual Life a Celebration
- Jump Jive: Aerobic Fitness through Dance
- Justice for All?: Strengths and Weaknesses in our System of Justice
- Just in Case: Tips on Emergency Preparedness (for Your Purse, Suitcase, Car, and Home)

- Karate for Fun, Fitness, and Defense
- Kayaking: Exploring the Waters
- Keeping Bees: A Deseret Tradition Lives On
- Keeping Learning Alive: Adult Education Opportunities in Our Community
- Keeping Up with Technology: What's the Latest in Our Digital World
- Kickboxing for Fun, Fitness, and Defense
- Kindergarten to College: Educating Our Children
- Kindness Begins at Home: Creating an Atmosphere of Kindness and Courtesy
- Kindred Spirits: Developing and Nourishing Friendships
- King Lear's Daughters: Examining the Women in Shakespeare's Famous Tragedy
- Kinship: Climbing around in Your Family Tree
- Kitchen Clutter Control: Defining and Organizing Work spaces in Your Kitchen
- Knaves, Knights, and Chivalry: Life and Love in the Middle Ages
- Kneady Women: Bread Baking for Fun, Food, and Therapy!
- Knick Knack Nuts: Collections to Share and Show Off
- Knitting, Knots, and Needles: Knitting and Handwork Basics
- Knot on Your Life!: Know How to Tie Up Everything on the Planet

- Langston Hughes, An African-American Poet
- Launching Out: Things You Need to Know when Starting Your Own Business
- Leadership Skills That Lift and Love
- Learning to Drive: Basics
- Learning to Forgive: Difficult Lessons toward Personal Freedom
- Leeches to Liposuction: Medical Treatments through the Ages
- Lemonade Stands and Paper Routes: Teaching Economics to Children
- Lending a Hand: Habitat for Humanity and Other Participatory Service Organizations
- Lessons from Kirtland
- Lessons on Love: Reflecting on 1 Corinthians 13
- Letting Go; Letting God: Releasing Ourselves from the Impulse to Control Everything
- Lip Service: Lip Balms and Oral Health Care
- Little Changes for Big Savings: Surprising Money-Saving Tips Everyone Should Try
- Living Abundantly: Cultivating Gratitude in All Things
- Living in the Moment: Thriving in an Uncertain World
- Living Large: Accommodating the Big and Tall
- Lovely, Luxurious—and Easy!—Lap Quilts
- Love's Labors: Childbirth Then and Now
- Lucy Mack Smith: The Life and Lessons from a Remarkable Woman
- Lullabies around the World

- Magic with Makeup: Secrets to Enhancing Your Best Look
- Magnetic Poetry: A Lively Workshop Making Art with Random Words
- Make Up Your Mind: Decision-Making Tips for Serious Wafflers
- Making Amends: What it Takes to Truly Heal
- Making Peace with Your Past: Turning Injuries into Wisdom
- Mammograms and Mastectomies: Essentials of Breast Health
- Marshmallows and Chocolate Bars: Essentials for Successful Campfires
- *A Marvelous Work and a Wonder*: Group Study of LeGrand Richard's LDS Classic
- Marvelous Marinades: Great Ideas for Giving Meat More Zing
- Marvelous Meals in a Matter of Minutes
- Merry Making: A Christmas Crafts Workshop
- The Merry Widow: Learning to Live Happily Alone Again
- Misery Loves Company: Breaking out of Relationships That Draw You Down
- Missionary Memories: Our Returned Sister Missionaries Share Their Stories
- Modesty in a Modern World
- Mommy Knows Best and Other Myths We Want Our Children to Believe
- My Child Can't Read: Advancing Literacy at Home
- Mystery Meals: Come Discuss this Month's Mystery over Lunch

+ Native Nature: Plants and Wildlife Unique to Our Area
+ The Natural Man . . . and Woman: The Human Condition and the Gift of the Atonement
+ Nauvoo: Heartache, History, and Heritage
+ Needles and Pins: Sewing for Beginners (for Intermediates, for the Advanced)
+ Needles and Pins: Textiles Then and Now—a Hands-On Workshop with Examples
+ Newlywed Woes: Seasoned Spouses Share Wisdom on Snags in New Marriages
+ New Strategies for Keeping Pace in our High-Tech World
+ New Ways of Thinking about Old Patterns: Changing Perspectives Can Change Lives
+ "Nice": Can We Sabotage our Strength by being "Nice" at all Costs?
+ Nobody Knows the Trouble I've Seen: Inviting Christ to Heal your Private Sorrows
+ No Place Like Home: Making Your Home a Welcoming Haven
+ Not Tonight, Dear: Stresses Affecting Intimacy in Marriage
+ Notable Female Leaders of the Restoration
+ Notable Musicians of the Church
+ Now or Never?: Strategies to Committing to Healthy Change
+ "Now That I Have Your Attention": What God Most Wants Us to Know and Understand
+ Nuts, Bolts, and Nails: Handy Uses for Little Hardware

- "O Say, What is Truth?": Founding Our Faith on the Basic Doctrines of the Gospel
- Oat Cuisine: Delicious Grain-based Dishes
- Occasionally an Idiot: Forgiving Ourselves and Others for Being Human
- Offering our All: Becoming a Real Disciple of Christ
- Offerings of Service: Making Creative Coupon Books for Many Occasions
- On the Other Hand: Learning to Appreciate Different Opinions
- One Elephant Went Out to Play: Repertoire of Tried and True Children's Songs
- One for All and All for One: Building a Zion Community
- One Size Does NOT Fit All: Fashion tips for All Body Types
- Only So Much You Can Do: Taking Care of *Your* Life When Others Want You to Fix Theirs
- Only When I Laugh: Humor as a Great Healing Tool
- Open Hearts, Busy Hands: Easy Service Projects for Humanitarian Aid
- Orange You Glad You Came?: Great Ideas for Citrus Fruit
- Orrin Porter Rockwell: Joseph Smith's Bodyguard, and Other Colorful Characters
- Open Sesame: Making Halvah and other East Indian Treats
- Our Achilles Heal: Fighting Temptations Designed for Us

- Over the River and through the Woods: Thanksgiving Traditions and Innovations
- Over the Seas to Zion: the Scandinavian and English Convert Migrations to Utah
- Overcoming Addictions: Support Groups for Sufferers and Family

- Painting Like the Old Masters: An Historical Approach to Oil Painting
- Pansies, Poppies, or Prairie Grass: Determining What Will Grow Best Where You Live
- Parables: Storytelling with Power and Purpose
- Party Planning for the Pea-Brained: Easy Tips and Treats for All Occasions
- The Physics of Everyday Life or How I Opened the Jar Myself
- Picture This: Basic Tips for Taking, Cropping, and Framing Great Photos
- Pig, Bear, and Chick Lit: Fairy Tales and Picture Books for Children
- Pinewood to Puberty: Tricks and Tactics for Raising Responsible Boys
- Pioneer Stock Pots: Great Soup and Stew Recipes
- Planter Paradise: Gorgeous Planters, Flower Boxes, and Patio Gardens
- Please and Thank You: The Lost Arts of Etiquette
- Plywood Palaces: Very Cool Dollhouses You Can Build
- Portraits: Capturing Likenesses in Oils, Pastel, and Pencil—a series
- Pouch Animals: The Wild World of Marsupials
- Practically Perfect in Every Way: Becoming "Whole" Instead of "Perfect"
- Prophets of the Latter-days: The Lives and Contributions of the Presidents of the Church
- Purpose in Life: Allowing the Gospel to Provide Satisfying, Spiritual Fulfillment
- The Pursuit of Peace: Inner Calm in a Tumultuous World

- Quad Exercises: New Approaches to Scripture Study
- Quahogs, Scallops, and Oysters: Tasty Treasures from the Sea
- Quaint and Collectible: Heirlooms in the Attic
- Quality Control: Making Family Choices about the Media
- Quasars, Black Holes, and Far Out Phenomena
- Queasy Tummies?: Home Remedies that Really Work
- Queens and Priestesses: Remembering our Potential Day by Day
- Quenchers: Summer Smoothies and Slushies
- Quick Breads and Cupcakes: Small Treats from the Oven
- Quick Cooking: Planning, Shopping, and Preparing Meals in Minutes
- Quick Fixes for Every Fashion Faux Pas
- Quiet Books to the Rescue!: Teaching Reverence with Felt and Flannel
- Quilt, Quilter, Quiltest: Quilts from Miniatures to King Size on Display
- Quilting Cabins: Log Cabins in Traditional and Contemporary Fabrics
- Quincy to CSI: Advances in Forensic Science
- Quitting Your Job: Knowing When You've had Enough or Need More
- Quizzing Cousins: Fun Questions to Connect Your Extended Family
- Quoth the Raven, "Nevermore!": Studying Edgar Allen Poe

- Rackets and Whackers: Tennis, Badminton, and other Net Sports
- Rags to Riches: Recycling Made Easy . . . and Profitable!
- Read 'em and Weep: Tenderhearted Stories of Compassion and Love
- Rebecca, Rachel, and Ruth: Understanding Old Testament Women
- Redeemed from What?: Exploring the Deep Basics of the Gospel
- Reel Life Stories: Great Biographies on Film
- Refresh, Renew, Relax: Learning to Take a Breather
- Rejections and Rewrites: the Realities of Life as a Writer
- Rejoice, the Lord is King!: Singing Hymns Like You Mean It
- Render unto Caesar: Tax Planning and Pointers
- Renewable Energy: Surprising Sources for Fueling Life
- Repentance and Prayer: A Powerful Pair
- Restoration Gospel Insights
- Rice? Nice!: Amazing Side Dishes with Rice
- Roping and Riding for Beginners
- Roses Bloom Beneath Our Feet?: Strategies for Surviving your Eternal Family
- Rose-Colored Glasses: Trying to See the Good around Us

- Sacred Celebrations: How Faiths around the World Celebrate Their Special Days
- Sad All the Time: The Facts of Depression—Even in Gospel-centered Homes and Hearts
- Salaries and Raises: Negotiating for What You're Worth
- Sand, Surf, and Shore: Waterfront Vacations for all Budgets
- Seasoned Travelers: Proven Travel Pointers from Packing to Taxis to Tipping
- Shake it Up!: Milk Shakes, Frappes, and Other Cold, Yummy Drinks
- She Sells Sea Shells: Tongue Twisters and Other Fun Word Plays
- Sisters in the Scriptures: What We Can Learn from the Named and Unnamed Women
- Sisters' Slumber Party: A "You Snooze, You Lose" Relief Society Overnighter
- Sleep Deprivation: What's a Mother to Do?

- Slugs, Snails, and Other Gross Things: Protecting Your Garden from Pests
- *Somebody* Has to Do It: Getting Those Gross Jobs Done
- The Song of the Righteous is a Prayer Unto Me: Emma Smith's Hymn Book
- Spare the Rod: Effective Alternatives to Corporal Punishment
- Spice It Up: Spices and Seasonings from around the World
- Stamp of Approval: Stamp Collecting and Appreciation for the Beginner
- Strollers and Car Seats: Comparing Makes and Models for Every Need
- Stuck on Stucco: New Ideas in Wall Treatments
- Sunshine and Safety: Protecting Ourselves from Skin Cancer
- Summer Time Free Fun: No Cost events in Our Community for All Ages

- Talents and Stewardship: Enjoying and Enhancing Our God-Given Gifts
- Tempting TVP and Tofu?: Delicious Meals from Bland Beginnings
- Ten Tips for Good Talks: Preparing and Presenting Better Sacrament Talks
- Thanksgiving: Not Just a Holiday in November
- Thriving with Diabetes
- Times and Seasons: Spreading News in Early Church History
- Toddlers, Tykes, and Terrible Twos: Lessons from and for the Little Ones
- Tossed, Diced, Chopped, and Gelled: Salads of All Varieties
- Tough Love and Tender Mercy: Knowing How to Set Limits with Your Loved Ones
- Trains, Planes, and Automobiles: Getting from Point A to Point B with Minimum Hassle
- Trees, Forests, and Fires: Safety Precautions in Wilderness Areas
- Trials and Tribulation: Whatever Happened to "Man is That He Might Have Joy?"
- Tribes across the Continent: Native Americans of the Northern Hemisphere
- Tricks up Your Sleeve: Illusions to Amaze and Entertain
- Tried and True: Maintaining a Marriage of Many Years
- Trumpets and Tympani: Glorious Band Instruments and Their Music
- Turning Hearts: Finding the Stories Behind the Facts and Figures
- Turning a Heel: Knitting Socks for Fun and Service

- Udderly Impossible: Coping with Milk Allergies
- Um . . . You Know . . . Like: Developing Precision in our Language
- Uncharted Territories: When We Find Ourselves in Crises We Couldn't Have Imagined
- Under the Hood: Becoming Familiar with the Innards of Your Car
- Under the Sea: Creatures of the Deep
- Under No Conditions: Deal Breakers in Relationships
- Under Your Bed and in Your Purse: What Your Messes Say about You
- Unguents, Ointments, and Poultices: Herbal Remedies That Work
- Unto Us a Child Is Born: Celebrating the Birth of the Savior
- Unusual Uses for Everyday Items
- Up above the World So High: Star Gazing for Beginners
- Up You Go: Rock Climbing for Beginners (Intermediates, Advanced)
- Upbeat Stories of Faith and Fun
- Upbraiding Your Daughters: Cool Hairdos They'll Love
- Urban Myths and Legends We Like to Believe
- Used or New: Trading, Selling, and Buying a Car
- Utensils for a Fine-Tuned Kitchen
- Utmost Value: Determining What Means Most in Our Lives

- Vagabond Outings: Day Trips for Wandering and Discovering
- Valentine's Day: Cards, Crafts, and Cookies for This Romantic Holiday
- Valley Girls: What Childhood Was Like in the Salt Lake Valley's Pioneer Period
- Vane Ambition: Weather Vanes and Yard Ornaments Old and New
- Variables We Can't Control: Learning to Roll with Life's Punches
- Variations on Gospel Themes: Short Talks by Sisters on (Faith, Peace, Joy)
- Vein Ambition: Helping and Healing Varicose Veins
- Vengeance Is Whose?: The Balance between Righteous Wrath and Forgiveness
- Ventriloquism: Basic Tips That Won't Make You Feel Like a Dummy
- Verbs, Nouns, and Adjectives: Grammar Basics You May Have Forgotten
- Verily, I Say Unto You: When Jesus Highlights Messages
- Vicar, Imam, Pastor, Priest: Religious Leaders in Other Faiths
- Victory through Chocolate: Finding and Giving Moral Support in Creative Ways
- Vim, Vigor, and Veggies: Lifestyle Changes for Healthy Eating
- Vintage Fashions: What Our Great-Great Grannies Wore from Top to Toe
- Violets, Orchids, and other High-Maintenance House Plants
- Vocal Villagers: Understanding and Contributing to Our Community Government

- Wads of Wires: Introduction to Household Electronics
- Waist Management: Flexibility Exercises for the Midsection
- Walking the Walk: Including God in Our Everyday Lives
- Waltz, Merengue, and Cha Cha Cha: Having a Ball with Ballroom Dancing
- Warm and Wonderful Breakfast Cakes and Rolls
- Water Fun for Little Ones
- Wild and Wooly: Spinning Yarn on a Spindle and Wheel
- Wilderness Lessons: What We Can Learn from Christ's Time in the Wilderness
- What Should I Do with My Life?: Life Guidance for All Stages of a Woman's Life
- When All Else Fails, Improvise!: Creative Problem Solving on the Home Front
- When Our Parents Were Young: Capturing Stories While We Can
- Where in the World?: Geography Lessons without Embarrassment
- Where Were You When I Needed You?: Dealing with Abandonment and Guilt
- Winter Fun That Won't Cost a Fortune
- Wimps No More: Strength Training for Health and Longevity
- Women of the Wild, Wild West
- Wonder Woman, R.I.P.: Giving Ourselves Permission to Be Human
- The Worldwide Webs We Weave: Designing Your Own Website

- X-ing Out Xenophobia: Loving Our Brothers and Sisters Around the World
- X-mas: Keeping Christ in Christmas
- X-O-X-O: Codes that Communicate
- X-rays and Radiation: New Advances in Radiology

- The Yeast You Can Do: Fun with Breads and Other Rising Baked Goods
- Yellowstone: A National Park or Another Planet?
- Yin, Yang, and the Gospel: Finding Balance in Our Lives
- Yogurt, Smoothies, and Other Cool, Soft Delights
- Yokemates: Sharing Our Burdens with the Savior
- You Gotta Have Heart: Cardiac Health and You
- You Said WHAT?: Developing Tact and Sensitivity
- Young and Restless: Making Life Decisions in Your Twenties
- Yuletide Traditions around the World
- Yurts, Tents, and Tipis: Living in the Great Outdoors

- Zebras, Giraffes, and Elephants: Animals of Africa
- Zephaniah, Haggai, and the Other Prophets of the Old Testament with Hard-to-Pronounce Names
- Zing, Zip, and Zest: Great Recipes with Citrus Peel Appeal
- Zion: Definitions through Time

Extra Resources for Good Measure

How Home, Family, and Personal Enrichment Is Working in the Real World:

Here are some examples from wise women around the country who are involved with the new guidelines for home, family, and personal enrichment. One is a Relief Society president. One is an enrichment counselor. One is an enrichment leader. One is a Relief Society sister who attends.

Sister Eve Adams, an anonymous Relief Society sister in Salt Lake City, shares her point of view as a participant:

When I heard the directive to hold enrichment quarterly, I felt this was a good thing. We have a large enrichment committee, and to say they work extremely hard is an understatement. They serve a meal each month; they attach invitations

111

to everyone's door (works of art); the programs are major productions. So I thought, "Yes, simplify!"

They formed smaller committees such as spiritual and
service. They have not cut down on meetings. In fact, I think
they have more now, counting weekday projects. As I see it,
the only thing they do quarterly is the lesson.

The activities offered are wonderful. The sisters get
together once a month to attend the temple. I would really like
to join that group, but I am not around during the day. They
formed a sewing class taught by an impressively talented sister.
I was thrilled when they offered that class in the evenings as
well as the day. The sewing secrets she shares are terrific, and
I do not want to miss any of her classes! (Her husband makes
the best cookies.)

This next Thursday evening is the monthly enrichment
meeting with a meal and babysitters provided. It's the high
priests' turn to babysit. We have several hundred children in
our ward—mostly under the age of three. Whenever it is the
high priests' turn, my husband is there. He dreads it. Don't
get me wrong, he loves children, but it is a monumental job
to corral so many children in such a small space for two and a
half hours. He does not feel enriched.

Our enrichment leaders have emphasized that they have
created many programs to try to reach the needs of every
sister, and we are not to feel guilty if we do not attend every
meeting. But I hate to miss because they work so hard; I need
to socialize more; the food is always so good. What happened
to simplify?

Nancy Harward, currently serving as Relief Society
enrichment counselor in the Montgomery Ward, Cincinnati
Ohio East Stake, shares these thorough observations:

Our ward had the advantage/disadvantage of having both
a new enrichment counselor and new enrichment leader called
in mid-November 2005. This didn't give us much time to prepare to implement a totally new program in January 2006

(especially since the holidays were upon us by the time we got going); but the advantage was that we could start completely new, with fresh ideas. The first thing we did was to schedule our four ward enrichment meetings for 2006. Once the holidays were over, we got our enrichment committee together (six other women) to brainstorm and divvy up general responsibilities. We also chose a general theme for each quarterly meeting: one would center on home, another on family, a third on personal enrichment, and the fourth on one of our ward welfare focus areas (this year, budgeting and finances). Next, we focused on a few high-priority activities to organize immediately. We were fortunate to have had a couple of women volunteer to spearhead these, so the Relief Society presidency and enrichment committee developed some guidelines and then turned over the responsibility to the volunteer coordinator.

The new system has the advantage of more flexibility than before. This allows us the ability to tactfully meet the urgent needs of a few women without trying to fit a particular class into a more general meeting. This flexibility provides more opportunities for women to socialize in settings other than church.

The main challenge for our enrichment committee has been trying to act on all the suggestions and requests we've received, deciding how many activities we can handle, and setting priorities. For example, there are a number of women in our ward who are interested in forming a scrapbooking group; there also are some women who could use instruction in planning for retirement. Do we allocate our resources toward the scrapbooking group because we know it would be well attended and thus would address the need for women to socialize? Or do we put our energy into organizing a retirement planning seminar that would probably draw fewer women but would address a more urgent need?

Another challenge is how to make sure that each woman in the ward is offered an appropriate opportunity to participate with a group every month. It's easy to provide activities for those who attend regularly, but it's harder to draw in the ones who tend to remain on the fringes.

Our first quarterly event was "Make 2006 a Happier, Healthier New Year." The evening began with a twenty-minute motivational lesson on safeguarding our physical health; participants then rotated through three twenty-minute sessions where they (1) reviewed principles of preventive health care, (2) received basic training on why and how to use hand weights, and (3) reviewed principles of good nutrition and made healthy snacks. Another event, "Enriching Relationships with Extended Family Members," is still in the planning stages, but will include ideas for organizing family reunions, strengthening ties with distant family members, and encouraging good communication across the generations.

Our ongoing activities include:

MOTHERS' SHARING TIME

This discussion group meets monthly on the night formerly designated as enrichment night, except in those months when a quarterly enrichment meeting is scheduled. The coordinator chooses a parenting topic for each meeting and arranges for a panel or speaker to get the ball rolling. The emphasis, however, is on mothers of all ages sharing experiences and ideas with each other. Sample topics are discipline, communicating with children, and grandparenting. This meeting is held at the church, and a member of the enrichment committee arranges for a nursery.

BOOK GROUP

This group meets monthly. Participants take turns choosing a book to read and discuss. The only problem we've run into with this one is that since the group carries the imprimatur of the Relief Society, the books we choose must be free of any material that some might consider "questionable"—not an easy task. We started out following the "Time Out for Women" book list, but because participants in our ward were disappointed by some of those selections, we decided to strike out on our own.

DAYTIME TEMPLE TRIP

This is one regularly scheduled day each month. Sisters who would like to attend call the temple to reserve a spot, and then they contact the ward coordinator who helps arrange carpools.

MONTHLY HOLIDAY LUNCH

Participating sisters take turns hosting an informal pot-luck lunch with an appropriate holiday theme (Valentine's Day, St. Patrick's Day, Cinco de Mayo). We're also trying to include ethnic-oriented celebrations so that people can share the traditions of their heritage.

MALL WALKERS

Participants meet at a local mall to walk in the morning before the stores open.

We came up with our ideas through brainstorming, responding to requests, and taking people up on offers to spearhead a particular activity. We also are in the process of doing a phone survey of the entire ward Relief Society, which we thought would garner more useful responses than a written survey. (This survey follows Sister Harward's comments.)

ADVANTAGES AND SNAGS

The obvious advantage is that instead of having to plan a monthly activity that will draw (and benefit) the maximum number of people, we can offer a greater variety of activities that can meet more individual needs. The obvious snag is trying to keep a lot more balls in the air. Instead of one monthly meeting, there is an infinite number of programs and activities we could be doing. How do you decide how much is enough?

PRIESTHOOD INVOLVEMENT

Our bishopric sees the enrichment program as a good means of helping the ward as a whole address various concerns. For example, our ward welfare committee established four focus areas for this year: physical health, emotional health, financial planning, and employment skills enhancement. The Relief Society is planning, or has already offered programs and activities that address specific topics within each of these focus areas.

Here is what Sister Harward distributed to prepare her Relief Society sisters for their survey:

> Dear Sisters,
>
> Within the next few weeks, you should receive a phone call from a member of the Montgomery Ward Relief Society enrichment committee. We will be conducting a survey to discover your needs and interests so that we can develop enrichment activities to provide opportunities to meet some of those needs and explore your interests with like-minded women.
>
> Questions will include:
> * **What skills would you like to learn or develop?**
>   Examples: Would you like to learn how to read music? Edit digital photographs? Communicate more effectively with teenagers?
> * **What subject areas would you like to learn more about?**
>   Examples: Would you like to learn more about preparing for retirement? Interesting places

to visit in and around Cincinnati? Alternatives for managing ADD?

- **What skills or knowledge do you have that you could share with others?**
    Examples: Could you teach
    someone how to crochet? Pre-
    pare tax forms? Make bagels?
    Line dance?

- **What activities would you like to participate in that you might enjoy more if you could share the experience with friends?**
    Examples: Would you like to
    join a group to attend a concert?
    Practice yoga? Serve a meal at a
    homeless shelter? Read scrip-
    tures?

- **What time of day and day of the week would you prefer to meet for enrichment activities?**

- **What needs do you have that the Montgomery Ward Relief Society could help fulfill?**
    Examples: I need a tennis part-
    ner. I need to talk with someone
    over the age of six more often. I
    need help to find a better job.

We really need your input so we can
serve you better. We hope you'll take a few
minutes to share your thoughts with us
when we call.

Thanks,
Nancy Harward
Enrichment Counselor
Montgomery Ward Relief Society

Here is the script for the telephone survey conducted in Sister Harward's ward.

Hello, my name is _____. I'm a member of the Montgomery Ward of the LDS Church. I'm also a member of the Relief Society enrichment committee. The purpose of this committee is to plan programs and activities for the women of the ward. In the past, we've held monthly enrichment meetings. Have you ever attended an enrichment meeting? If you have, you know that these have included a variety of lessons and activities—anything from Bible study to budgeting to making bubbling bath salts. These events have been informative and fun—but we think we can do better.

This year we're changing the structure of the enrichment program, making it more flexible so that we can better meet the needs of the women in our ward. Instead of having just one monthly weeknight meeting, we're planning a variety of activities at a variety of times. The reason I'm calling is to find out what kinds of activities we can plan for *you*. Do you mind answering a few questions to help us improve our enrichment program? (See the questions on the previous letter.)

These observations are from **Michelle Purrington**, the Relief Society president in the Weston First Ward of the Boston Massachusetts Stake.

Here's how we have gone about organizing enrichment activity groups. It is not clear to me what groups will ultimately have staying power.

1. The first thing we did was collect an e-mail address for every sister in the ward. We rely heavily on e-mail; this keeps the announcements before Relief Society meetings to a minimum. This is critical with so many activities going on.

2. The enrichment committee then came up with broad topics (exercise group, outing group) and invited the sisters to sign up for these through e-mail. We also sent hard copies around on Sunday, but found nearly everyone had already signed up through e-mail. We found that once we had this

framework in place, the sisters began to organize themselves through our e-mail system. For instance, a sister who is a kick-boxing instructor stepped forward and offered kickboxing at the church. Another sister offered to lead walks through the many trails we have in the area. We are also in the process of forming a gourmet group (theme lunches with specific recipe assignments) that has received a lot of interest.

3. We scouted around for a group leader. A few women proactively offered. For other groups, we recruited "organiz-ers" who were simply in charge of the first get together, and then passed off the responsibility to a new volunteer in the group. Members of the enrichment committee keep loose tabs on what is going on with specific groups, nudging along and making sure upcoming events are posted in the newsletter.

4. The enrichment committee formed separate e-mail groupings for sisters interested in specific groups (a craft group e-mail list), so upcoming events only go to women interested in crafting. Otherwise we would be overrun with e-mails! We have a Relief Society Newsletter that goes out once a month. Upcoming activities are always posted in the newsletter. This gives everyone an opportunity to know what is going on in the event someone new would like to join.

We see our role as leaders as providing the framework (e-mail lists, newsletter, designated leader), but we feel it is up to the women in the ward to develop these groups. The groups exist for their growth, pleasure, and entertainment and are not intended to be yet another church obligation they are compelled to "support."

Kerstin Bean, enrichment Leader in the North Shore First Ward, Wilmette Illinois Stake, shares her experiences and written survey.

With the new guidelines, we felt that the general Relief Society wanted to give the wards more flexibility and give sisters more time to spend with family. As a result, we really wanted:

+ To understand the needs of our sisters more so we could form activities and meetings that would meet their needs and wants. What types of activities should we do that will help the sisters build friendships?
+ To determine what types of groups sisters would be *genuinely* interested in coming to, not just because they feel they have to support a church-sponsored activity.
+ To create a way outside of Relief Society where sisters could gather, enjoy each other, and learn new hobbies or reach their goals all at once.

I include the survey we used in the North Shore First Ward. I took the format from a survey we used in my previous ward. All the information on the survey, however, came from ideas we came up with as an enrichment committee. On the survey, we tried to include activities that all types of people would be interested in—artsy, physically fit, or spiritual.

We are still learning as a committee what works and what doesn't. What is too much—and there definitely can be too much—and what is not enough. We figure if there are a few sisters interested, great! That is enough to start a group. The point is to meet the needs of individuals. Even if there are only three women walking together as a result of a fitness group, or four women supporting a knitting group, those three or four women are getting their needs met or else they wouldn't be participating.

If we have an excited, organized group leader for each of the interest groups, the groups seem to be a success. Also we figure that finding the right activity is key—if we pick the right things to do, we will have sisters participating.

Name: _____

This interests me	Possible Enrichment Activities	I could lead this
	I would like to meet weekly, every other week, or by group e-mail to share insights from the ward's communal reading of the Book of Mormon.	
	I would like to join other sisters in the following fitness activities (circle all that apply): Swimming Walking Jogging Hiking Biking Training for a race Tennis Aerobics	
	I am interested in learning what's available at the Family History Center.	

This **interests** me	Possible Enrichment Activities	I could **lead** this
	I would want to join a mom's support group to discuss parenting skills such as: constructive discipline, teaching children about sexuality, issues presented by special needs and gifted children, how to find joy in motherhood.	
	I would like to know more about depression and other mental health issues.	
	I would like to be part of a group that tries out new restaurants every month.	
	I want to do hands-on volunteer work in the community—with a shelter, food bank, or other service organization.	

This interests me	Possible Enrichment Activities	I could lead this
	I could use a class on time management skills.	
	I would like to go on field trips around the Evanston and Chicago area (Art Institute, Field Museum, Science and Industry, Shedd Aquarium, Adler Planetarium, Block Gallery, Frank Lloyd Wright homes in Oak Park, Graceland Cemetery, Michigan Avenue, Kohl Children's Museum, Chicago Children's Museum).	

Other Resources to Explore:

Ancestry magazine
Backyard Living magazine
Cooking Light magazine
Ensign, New Era, and *The Friend* magazines
Family Circle magazine
Family Fun magazine
LDS Living
Martha Stewart Living magazine
Parents magazine
Raspberries & Relevance: Enrichment in the Real World, compiled by
    Linda Hoffman Kimball, CFI, 2004
Real Simple magazine
Working Mother magazine
www.lds.org – Provident Living link
www.lds.org – Serving in the Church, Relief Society link

About the Author

Since Linda Hoffman Kimball wrote this book, she has alphabetized every CD, DVD, canned good, and magazine in her house. She is an artist, a poet, a columnist for an online interfaith magazine (www.beliefnet.com), the author of two humorous novels, *Home to Roost* and *The Marketing of Sister B.*; and a picture book for children, *Come with Me on Halloween*. This is her fourth book for Cedar Fort. She and her husband, Christian, have three mostly grown children. She is the Relief Society president in the North Shore First Ward in the Wilmette Illinois Stake.